Taking Technical Risks

Taking Technical Risks

How Innovators, Executives, and Investors Manage High-Tech Risks

Lewis M. Branscomb and Philip E. Auerswald

with contributed essays by

Henry Chesbrough and Richard S. Rosenbloom
George C. Hartmann and Mark B. Myers
Mary L. Good
James C. McGroddy
F. M. Scherer and Dietmar Harhoff

The MIT Press, Cambridge, Massachusetts, and London, England

Library of Congress Cataloging-in-Publication Data

Branscomb, Lewis M., 1926– .
  Taking technical risks : how innovators, executives, and investors manage high-tech risks / Lewis M. Branscomb and Philip E. Auerswald ; with contributed essays by Henry Chesbrough . . . [et al.]
    p.   cm.
  Includes bibliographical references and index.
  ISBN 0-262-02490-X (hc. : alk. paper)
  1. Risk management. 2. Technological innovations. I. Auerswald, Philip E.
  II. Title.

HD61 .B73 2001
658.5—dc21   00-049620

Contents

Preface

This book is the result of a joint Harvard-MIT Project on Managing Technical Risk, sponsored by the Advanced Technology Program (ATP) of the National Institute for Standards and Technology (NIST). The project sponsor at NIST, Darin Boville, was an active participant in every stage of its conception and conduct.

In the spring of 1999, Lewis Branscomb, the principal investigator for the project, and Kenneth Morse, Managing Director of the MIT Entrepreneurship Center, invited a group of experienced practitioners and academic experts to two workshops on the management of technical risk. At the first, held at MIT's Sloan School on June 22, 1999, the practitioners shared their experiences and two detailed case studies of high-tech innovation, prepared by the MIT and Harvard Business School entrepreneurship programs under the guidance of Michael Roberts, were evaluated with the help of innovators and investors from the subject firms. Summaries of the discussion were made available to all participants.

A second workshop was held on September 17, 1999. Academic participants and practitioners presented commissioned papers, which were subsequently reviewed by the leadership team and the consulting editor, Teresa Lawson. All authors were then given the opportunity to revise their contributions to address issues raised during the review process. References in the present book to workshop discussions are to the 1999 project.

We have drawn heavily on the Report to NIST-ATP entitled *Managing Technical Risk: Understanding Private Sector Decision Making on Early Stage, Technology-Based Projects,* by Lewis M. Branscomb, Kenneth Morse, and Michael Roberts. This report is available from the NIST website: <http://www.atp.nist.gov/eao/gcr_787.pdf>. It contains two main sections: (i) the report of the project team, and (ii) the collection of commissioned papers. Both sections of the report are intended to complement, rather than substitute for, surveys and statistical studies of a more representative nature. Its purpose, like that of the present book, is to open up the subject to discussion, in the hope that technical innovators, business executives, venture investors, and government R&D officials will all become more aware of how the other groups think about the question of technical risk management and the way this affects their own activities.

Both our original study for the ATP and the present volume aim to inform the decisions of government managers and private entrepreneurs by exploring how the technical dimensions of business risk are viewed and managed by innovators, business executives, and venture investors. Our hope is that our work will deepen understanding of the risks in science-based innovation, enabling ATP and similar programs to be further strengthened.

This book takes the form of an essay by Lewis M. Branscomb and Philip E. Auerswald. For expert opinions and observations the book relies primarily on the workshops as described in the ATP Report. Thus all of the direct quotes of participants in the project workshops come, with their consent, from the record of those workshops and the published report. Any direct quotations not having their origin in the project are separately attributed.

Between the chapters we have included some of the commissioned papers from the project, selected to provide the authors' unique insights into the issues we discuss. The chapters, though, are self-contained, so that they can be read sequentially without the contributed essays. We are deeply indebted to the authors of the essays, who also participated in the workshops and provided valuable advice on the project. We are particularly indebted to Professors F. Michael Scherer and Josh Lerner, not only for the depth of work we have cited but for much good advice based on their expertise in this field of scholarship.

We gratefully acknowledge the important contribution that our colleagues Kenneth Morse and Michael Roberts made to this project and to the ideas in this book. To Michael Roberts we owe a special thanks for his preparation of the discussion on two cases published by Harvard Business School. The discussion of the firms AIR and Trexel in this book was largely authored by him. Finbarr Livesey at the Kennedy School of Government contributed research for the book and provided insightful comments on the manuscript. We are pleased to thank Beth Mathisen and Nora O'Neil for their administrative support. Our consulting editor, Lois Malone, contributed much to the clarity of this manuscript.

Introduction

A book about risk is necessarily a book about boundaries: boundaries between an action contemplated and an action taken, between what is known and what is not known, and between events that can be controlled and events that cannot. This book is no exception. Our objective is to map the very specific boundary that lies between invention (an idea) and innovation (a product). It is a space in which engineers, managers, economists, policy makers, and even venture capitalists all feel uncomfortable; a space occupied by academic-entrepreneurs and seed funds, incubators and "excubators," technology bureaucrats and angels.

The boundary between invention and innovation is the place where individual human ingenuity connects with long-term macroeconomic growth.[1] There, concepts become prototypes; teams become companies; today's technical breakthroughs become tomorrow's goods, services, and economic infrastructure. This is particularly true for those technical advances that promise to open up new markets or that may destabilize existing markets. These radical innovations, illustrated by the upper right-hand quadrant in Figure 1, carry the highest technical risks. But they also carry the highest market risk, for demand is particularly uncertain. These innovations are often approached through the creation of new firms, which, as we shall see, are often the chosen instruments for commercialization of science-based discoveries.

This book does not confine itself to radical innovations, but focuses on the top two quadrants in Figure 1, dealing with the risks

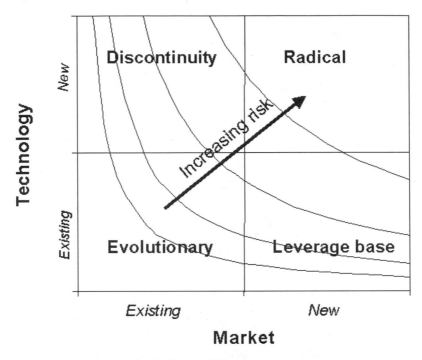

Figure 1 Quadrants of risk. The solid lines represent constant overall risk.

associated with those innovations that are based on new technology. Innovations in the lower left quadrant represent the lowest risk; market risks dominate in the lower right quadrant.

Specifically, in this book we ask:

- In the United States today, who takes technical risks? How do the varying objectives of participants in the innovation system—technologists, investors, managers—affect the assessment of risk?

- Are there systematic gaps in sources of finance, types of research required, or trust between innovators and investors/managers that must be overcome in the process of turning inventions into innovations?

- To what extent is technical risk—the risk that a product won't work—separable from market risk—the risk that a product won't sell?

- What institutions in the U.S. economy support taking technical risks? How do they support it?
- What is the appropriate role of government in supporting taking technical risks in commercial innovations?
- What long-term institutional and technological trends affect the ability of key actors to take and overcome technical risks?

Throughout this book our focus is primarily on understanding the behavior of individuals and institutions, and only secondarily on interpreting statistical evidence. Several themes will be explored and developed:

- *Successful innovations are rare, and the rewards must compensate for the risks.* Successful innovations are statistically rare, yet both innovation and sustained growth in the future depend on the regular occurrence of innovation today. Risk and uncertainty are inherent in the nature of high-tech innovation. This is true not only because high-tech innovation uses new and immature science as its tool and seeks to create the demand that it must then satisfy, but also because it seeks to destabilize markets and produce unusually favorably returns. A central theme of the book is the tension between the rarity of successful innovations and the economic need for institutionalizing their creation.
- *There are many ways to fail: Technical risks and market risks are closely related.* Technical uncertainties are not determined by the vagaries of nature alone, but are dependent on available knowledge about markets, since technology will determine available product specifications, which in turn are constrained by acceptable market opportunities. Thus technical and market risks are not clearly separable. For a given level of technical knowledge, the more one knows about markets, the lower the technical risk.
- *Innovation systems are the key to resolving the tension between the rarity of successful innovation and the need for a dependable sequence of innovations.* Innovation systems exist on intersecting scales—including the corporation, the city/region, the nation, and the transnational region—and may be quite different for different technologies. This is why *institutions* (stable networks of incentives/contracts/trust) are important.

- *There are serious financial, technological, and institutional gaps in the U.S. system of innovation.* These gaps create additional risk to innovators seeking to convert science-based inventions to commercializable products and processes. These, taken together, can be called shortcomings in social and public capital for innovation.

- *The pace of development is accelerating and is changing the innovation system.* With advances in science and engineering, increased global competition, and decreasing product cycle times, innovators must learn to reduce market and technical risks concurrently. Thus the linear model of innovation, known to be inappropriate for the evolutionary progress that characterizes most of industry, is increasingly inappropriate for radical, science-based innovations as well.

- *Governmental institutions, state and federal, must be seen as part of the fabric of social capital on which the innovation system rests.* Government should no longer be seen only as a mechanism for selective, limited interventions in case of egregious market failures. Except for a major role in the funding of research, this role will be an indirect, enabling one, but no less important for that fact.

While this volume addresses many of the core themes pertinent to "taking technical risks," it does not seek to address them all. To begin with, we do not address the environmental, security, or other risks related to the creation or use of new technology.[2] By "technical risk" we refer only to the possibility of failure in the attempt to convert an invention into an innovation (as when the product does not meet specifications in terms of performance, cost of production, or reliability). Second, we focus our analysis on the U.S. innovation system, excluding discussion of other national innovation systems and of global innovation networks. Of course, the issues we address do have relevance to innovation systems in other countries (particularly industrial democracies); but our presentation and discussion of policy implications are specific to this country. Third, we do not address the important and complex intellectual property issues involved in early-stage technology-based innovation. While we recognize that intellectual property rights (IPR) play a large role in the management of business risks in science-based innovation (particularly in biotechnology and software), we avoid discussing them both because these are treated thoroughly elsewhere,[3] and because we seek to emphasize the distinctly behavioral and institutional factors affecting the taking of technical risks. Finally, our approach is descriptive rather than theoretical. We neither build nor describe formal models of technical risk, uncertainty, and innovation.[4] Instead, we gather from practitioners and from the relevant academic literature the best judgments on the process of early-stage, technology-based innovation to inform innovators, investors, managers, public policy scholars, and government officials.

The structure of the book is as follows. Chapter I explores the connection between invention and innovation. Who takes the risks, and how do inventors, managers, and investors think about success and failure? In Chapter II we explore what we mean by technical risk-taking, how firms might try to quantify risks, and the extent to which technical risk cannot be quantified independent of market risks. Chapter III deals with institutional differences. Why do large, medium-sized, and new firms approach technical risk-taking so differently? How might firms of different size and maturity look to relationships outside the firm, for example with university researchers, to overcome some of their disadvantages? Chapter IV explores the strategies for managing risk both by investors and by firms. It asks whether portfolio strategies are a reasonable way to deal with technical risk, and takes us through two case studies of firms that were created specifically to exploit radical inventions. Chapter V takes us outside the firm to investigate the general sources of risk in high-tech innovation and what public policy can do to mitigate risks, especially in the case of radical innovations that might have great benefits to society over time. Finally, in Chapter VI we consider the future. Because long-term economic growth at regional, national, and global scales will be driven increasingly by sustained technological innovation, inventors, managers, and investors alike will continue to be under pressure to turn technological breakthroughs rapidly into market-ready products. Among the core responsibilities of government will therefore be the cultivation of an environment in which actors in the innovation system can successfully take, and overcome, technical risks.

Between the chapters are contributed essays, each of which offers a practitioner's or an academic's perspective on the ideas discussed. The first essay, "Technical Risk, Product Specifications, and Market Risk," was written by George Hartmann and Mark Myers of the Xerox Corporation. They describe one of the most well developed methodologies for measuring as well as managing the technical component of business risk.

The second essay, "The Dual-Edged Role of the Business Model in Leveraging Corporate Technology Investments" by Henry Chesbrough and Richard Rosenbloom, points out that innovations must take place within business models that may call for a level of adaptability many business executives lack.

The third essay, Jim McGroddy's "Raising Mice in the Elephants' Cage," shares the experience of attempting radical innovations in a large, successful corporation.

The fourth essay, "Technology Policy for a World of Skew-Distributed Outcomes" by F. M. Scherer and Dietmar Harhoff, is reprinted from *Research Policy* by permission of the publisher. This paper demonstrates the limitations of relying on averaging one's returns across a portfolio of risky investments, giving weight to a basic conclusion of this book: There is no substitute for skill, knowledge, and courage in ensuring a safe crossing of the gap between invention and innovation.

The last essay is by Mary Good, who, as Undersecretary for Technology in the Department of Commerce, was responsible for government programs to help commercial firms reduce the risks of radical innovations when the latter would serve the economy. Her essay, "Will Industry Fund the Science and Technology Base for the Twenty-First Century?," asks if there is a legitimate role for government as product cycles shorten and technical and market risks merge.

As the first chapter explains, this book is about unlikely events. It is a story of dreamers and doers, risking their own fortunes or those of others equally eager for the brass ring of fortune, trying to extract from the extraordinary richness of scientific knowledge the opportunity to create new products and services. In our narrative we have relied to a substantial degree on the experience of practitioners in the art of technical risk-taking: the inventors, business managers, and venture investors. Our story of the risks in innovation is their story; to a significant extent they will tell it in their own words.

Notes

1. Inventions are original, non-obvious and useful creations of the mind, intended to be sufficiently promising commercially that they will motivate the inventor to see the invention produced and marketed. Innovations are products or services, new to the producer, that have been successfully introduced into the market. (See Chapter VI, note 3.)

2. See, for example, Joy (2000).

3. Jaffe (2000) provides a survey of both the history of U.S. patent policy and the academic literature attempting to measure the impacts on innovation of changes in patent policy.

4. For examples see Evenson and Kislev (2000), Baumol (1993), Aghion and Tirole (1994), and Auerswald et al. (2000). Laffont (1990) provides an introduction to the formal theory of uncertainty and information. An approach to R&D decision-making based on real options theory is introduced in Amram and Kulatilaka (1999) and more formally described in Huchzermeier and Loch (1999).

I

Between Invention and Innovation

Despite its importance both to business and growth, the boundary between invention and innovation has not been a focal point of study in business schools, departments of economics, or science policy programs. Pre-competitive research is, by definition, not quite business. Accordingly, business school case studies most often start after an invention has already been turned into an innovation: when the specifications for a good or service have been established, and a target market defined. At the same time, the detailed process by which profit-seeking actors turn inventions into innovations—with all its institutional and behavioral complexity—does not lend itself easily to either formal economic modeling or statistical analysis. Consequently, among economists only the specialized few have tended to take the sort of fine-grained approach to the study of the innovation process needed to explore the transformation of an idea into a product. Finally, studies in science policy usually stop at the point at which a commercial idea emerges from a work of scientific research.

The transition from invention to innovation is integrally linked to the anticipation of *profit* in the economic sense—returns in a particular activity above what could be earned using the same resources (management, capital, labor) in another activity. Simply put: Why go to the trouble of taking new science and turning it into a product in the first place? If you're the CEO of a Fortune 500 company, why not just take the resources you would have put into spinning new products out of your R&D labs and, instead, just hire twenty more sales people? You know already that most of the new products you develop will either function poorly, cost too much to produce, lag behind the competition, or just inexplicably fail to catch on. If you're an assistant professor of chemical engineering at a prestigious university, why not just focus on getting tenure instead of taking the risk of failure in a new venture? And if you're a prospective investor into a venture capital "seed" fund (one directed toward nascent ventures), why not just play it safe and buy U.S. Treasury bonds? The answer, obviously in every case, is that risky courses of action are undertaken because the relevant actors perceive the *possibility* of abnormally high returns. The risk must be matched by the prize. In this sense, profits drive the transition from invention to innovation.

Analysis of the relationship between profit, risk, uncertainty, and entrepreneurship is the subject of some of the classic works in economics (notably Knight 1921; Schumpeter 1912, 1942; and Kirzner 1973). Four decades of work by industrial economists on the subject has greatly expanded our understanding of the determinant of firm profitability.[1] Recent work on entrepreneuship (Baumol 1993) and venture capital (Gompers and Lerner 1999) has further added to our understanding of these critical economic phenomena. Yet, in a fundamental sense, profit plays only a marginal role in economics, both applied and theoretical. Applied economists are interested first and foremost in identifying statistical regularities, not in exhaustively analyzing factors that might have been responsible for a particular statistical "outlier"—a rare event that deviates from the norm, of which exceptional profits from an innovation are an example.[2] To economic theorists, extraordinary profits in a more or less competitive market represent either a disequilibrium (or "transient") phenomenon that will vanish as new firms enter to share in the opportunity, or some sort of lucky draw from a random distribution of firm outcomes. The situation is succinctly described in a interview with Zvi Griliches, the eminent Harvard economist of technological change, posthumously published in the *Journal of Economic Perspectives* (Kruger and Taylor 2000). Speaking in reference to his path-breaking work on the diffusion of agricultural innovations, Griliches observed:

When something new happens, things change, and now you go through some process in which a new equilibrium is established. That's going to take some time. We [economists] never had had a good theory of transition. And the field, by and large, moved toward an interpretation where everything is in equilibrium all the time.... There's very little discussion [in the literature] of the difference between what's on the [technological] frontier and what's the average. Somehow the average is interpreted as the frontier.... [W]hat's wrong with economics—not with the modeling economics, but sort of in applying the models to reality— is that everyone knows what to maximize.... There are no dollar bills lying on the sidewalk. In fact, all these guys who are jumping into the Internet, presumably they see a whole bunch of dollar bills out there.

A scholar with a half-century of studying technology and economic systems, Griliches reminds us that in the boundary between one equilibrium and the next is a transition. If the transition is long one (from the perspective of those in the system), it may be an important phenomenon to study. Furthermore, transitions are inherently related to opportunity and risk—the possibility of exceptional profits weighed against the likelihood of pedestrian failure. Technological frontiers thus should not be confused with averages.

The metaphor of the frontier is an apt one in more ways than one. Clearly, the technological frontier represents today what the "unexplored wilderness" of the New World did to European settlers on this continent.[3] Just as the European exploration and settlement of this continent proceeded in roughly coordinated stages—driven at once by competition and cooperation—so does current technological search and innovation proceed today in a haphazard synchrony of effort. Just as large, risky investments (by both governments and private individuals) were required to advance the boundaries of knowledge in the seventeenth and eighteenth centuries, so are such investments necessary today. Today's investments by government—state and federal—must support the basic scientific and technological research, much of it carried out in the research universities where the key talents are developed in support of discovery, invention and innovation. In addition, government policies must enhance the social, economic, and institutional infrastructure within which the private sector provides the innovation.

The power of the frontier image is such that the particular set of institutional and behavioral challenges faced by would-be innovators seeking to make the transition from scientific breakthrough to market-ready prototype is routinely referred to as the "Valley of Death."[4] In the next section we look further at this "Valley," discussing the gaps in funding, research, and information/trust by which it is defined. We find that taking technical risks means not only having the perseverance to attack difficult technical challenges with uncertain payoffs, but also finding strategies that bridge these institutional and behavioral gaps.

> "[T]he limited resources of the federal government, and thus the need for the government to focus on its irreplaceable role in funding basic research, has led to a widening gap between federally-funded basic research and industry-funded applied research and development. This gap, which has always existed but is becoming wider and deeper, has been referred to as the 'Valley of Death.' A number of mechanisms are needed to help span this Valley and should be considered." (Ehlers 1998)

From Scientific Breakthrough to Market-Ready Prototype: Crossing the "Valley of Death"

In the late 1980s, the stimulus of Cold War military R&D was fading. Low-cost, high-quality Asian production was eroding U.S. high-tech markets. Policy makers and corporate leaders alike were persuaded that sustained economic growth in the United States required domestic firms not only to improve their productivity, but also to improve their systems for innovating new products and processes. Academic analysts offered evidence that firms were systematically under-investing in leading-edge technologies and failing effectively to commercialize the products of their own research activities (Dertouzos, Solow, and Lester 1989; Tassey 1999).

These concerns, buttressed by theory pointing to a potential market failure in the area of early-stage technological developments, motivated new proposals for the role of government in the innovation system. These proposals were aimed at helping technical innovators bridge the gaps in institutional support between a scientific breakthrough and a market-ready prototype.

We can think of this Valley of Death as comprising three fundamental and interrelated gaps:[5]

- *Financial gap.* The gap between the research funds (typically from personal assets, government agencies, or corporate research) that support both the creation of the idea and the initial demonstration that it works, and the investment funds to turn the idea into a market-ready prototype (implying confidence in product specifications, knowledge of production costs, and identification of adequate markets). Typically, few sources of funding are available to aspiring innovators seeking to bridge this gap. They include "angel" investors (wealthy individuals, often personally experienced in creating new companies and/or developing new products); venture capital firms specialized in early-stage, or "seed" investments; military or other public procurement; and state or federal government programs specifically constructed for the purpose.

- *Research gap.* Initially an innovator demonstrates *to his or her own satisfaction* that a given scientific or technical breakthrough forms the basis for as commercial product. Subsequently, however, a substantial amount of difficult and potentially costly research (sometimes many years' worth) is needed before the envisioned product is transformed into a commercial reality with sufficient function, low enough cost, and high enough quality to survive competition in the marketplace.

- *Information and trust gap.* On each side of the Valley of Death stands a quite different archetypal character: the technologist on one side, and the investor/manager on the other. Each has different training, expectations, information sources, and modes of expression. The technologist knows what is scientifically interesting, what is technically feasible, and what is fundamentally novel in the approach proposed. In the event of failure, the technologist risks a loss of reputation, as well as foregone pecuniary returns. The investor/manager knows about the process of bringing new products to market, but will likely have to trust the technologist when it comes to technical particulars of the project in question. The investor/manager is generally risking other people's money. To the extent that technologist and investor/manager do not fully trust one another or cannot communicate effectively, the Valley of Death between invention and innovation becomes deeper still.

Two Cases of New Firm Creation

To illustrate the hazards inherent in attempts to convert a good idea for a science-based innovation into a product ready for development, production, and sale, we present two case studies of high-tech innovations. These case studies were conducted by Harvard Business School in cooperation with the MIT Sloan School's Entrepreneurship Center (Roberts and Lieb 1999; Roberts and Gardner 1999).

The first case—Advanced Inhalation Research—involves an invention that promised a better way to deliver medication to the lungs, through the inhalation of large but light particles. The science was solid enough to merit publication in top journals, yet years passed from the time of publication and patent filings to the time when the technology was ready for exploitation by a new, venture-funded company. The second case—Trexel, Inc.—involves a new way to manufacture stronger, cheaper, lighter plastic material. Again, despite access to leading-edge, proprietary technology and the involvement of a leading scientist, the interval from invention to innovation was ten years. Could the technical component of business risk have been reduced to an acceptable level in a period shorter than a decade? Alex d'Arbeloff, chairman of the MIT Corporation and an investor in Trexel, notes that "technical risk was inherent in the many issues that only arose when an application idea was pursued." The research gap is created in part by the inevitable interdependence of the technology and its market application.

Advanced Inhalation Research (AIR)

David Edwards was a postdoctoral fellow in chemical engineering at MIT in 1994 when he and his professor, Robert Langer, had an idea for a method of delivering drugs through inhalation into the lungs. Inhalation was not a new idea; it was already used to administer protein-based drugs that, if taken by mouth, would be destroyed by the body's digestive system. Edwards's idea was to use a new kind of carrier particle that would deliver the drug over a longer period of time, requiring a lower total dosage. No one had inhaled such particles before. Could Edwards make them? If inhaled, would they work, and would the method be safe? Many of the technical questions faced, after the initial invention in 1994, related to the breadth of application. How many different kinds of drugs could be delivered? The key question was, would the method provide sustained action, without the lungs clearing out the particles? Edwards said, "I always thought it would work. But will patents [to protect the idea] issue?"

Three years later, in 1997, Edwards's mentor, Professor Langer— a prolific innovator who had started many successful companies based on revolutionary biomedical ideas—put him in touch with Terry McGuire, a venture investor with whom Langer had worked before. McGuire agreed to invest $250,000 for 11 percent of a new company, Advanced Inhalation Research (AIR), and to act as the temporary CEO. By the spring of 1999, Edwards and McGuire felt they could sell the company for $100 million, only 18 months after starting AIR (but five years after Edwards had had the original technical idea on which the firm was based).

What happened between the invention of 1994 and the financial success of the new firm in 1999? Edwards knew that the original scientific idea was just the beginning and that he had to prove out the technology. During this period he moved from MIT to Pennsylvania State University, where he had been offered a faculty position and where the work continued, as he describes:

I was performing research on phagocytosis—the process through which microphages cleanse the lung of foreign particles—and realized that a larger particle would have a much better chance of remaining in the lung for a long period of time, and thus accomplish the sustained release of the drug. But I knew that the particle would need to be light in order to make it all the way into the deep lung. This was the key insight—a large but light particle. It was December 1994, one month before I planned to leave Langer's lab at MIT and move to Penn State University where I had been offered a faculty appointment.... It turned out that another student in Langer's lab was trying to make a similar particle that could encapsulate DNA. All of a sudden it hit me—this could actually be possible!

This was the "Eureka" moment. But where would the money come from to prove the idea was commercially practical? Edwards describes what happened:[6]

The early porous particle research was "bootlegged" or paid for by my "start-up" money at Penn State. Boot-legged in the sense that people— like Bob Langer, or people in his lab, threw in their time when they weren't working on things they were actually being paid for. As a new professor I had several hundred thousand (I forget the figure) dollars to get my lab started and I used some of this on the project. I did write a NIH grant, which got shot down precisely for the "porous particle aim" which … was viewed as "the weakest [part] of the proposal."

Soon Edwards had a lab established at Penn State and a joint Penn State–MIT project established. By the summer of 1995 the two teams had made the lactose-based particles and had shown that, being large and light, they were much more efficient and remained active in the lung longer than those of conventional aerosol inhalers. Edwards and Langer approached Inhale Thera-peutics, a public company in the drug delivery business, to see if they wanted to buy the technology. "They were interested," Edwards recalls, "but wanted us to come back when the technology was more advanced…. So for the next year we performed more animal studies, with insulin, and collected additional data. I traveled back to Langer's lab in Boston about once a month over the ensuing two years. By the end of that time, it was clear to us that the technology basically worked."

Edwards then wrote an article about their work for *Science* maga-zine, which appeared in June 1997. This was very well received and helped greatly to validate their work in the eyes not only of other scientists but of firms and investors as well. They had demonstrated "proof of concept"; they knew the idea would work.

The next step was to find the resources to move to commercial-ization. This was when they approached Terry McGuire, who knew and admired Langer and on the strength of that relationship visited Edwards at Penn State. McGuire describes the risks he saw in the investment:

[W]hen Bob [Langer] first approached me about investing in AIR, I made a few telephone calls. Everyone in the industry had the same response: there are a lot of successful drug delivery companies currently in the market…. Why do we need another one? The story was very easy to pass up. It was so early and there were still so many risks—so many ways it could go wrong. I put off Bob *twice* before I finally made the decision to take a hard look at the technology.

Edwards, Langer, and McGuire founded the company in May 1997. McGuire invested $250,000 for an 11 percent stake; he also agreed to act as temporary CEO. AIR then partnered with a succession of major drug companies, including Eli Lilly and Pfizer. In December 1998, AIR's IND was approved by the government, and Phase I clinical trials could begin. In March 1998 AIR received its first serious capital: $1 million for product development. AIR had made the perilous trip across the "Valley of Death." It was ready to face the risks associated with government approvals, medical acceptance, and competitive challenge.

Most of the purely technical risks had been resolved before Edwards left academia. Much of the research performed at Penn State and at MIT was supported by university funds or government research grants. The two universities clearly went further down the risk curve than would have been typical in the past. They were, of course, rewarded with equity and royalties in the deal. The first venture capital money came in two months after the *Science* article was published.

AIR had navigated the financial gap through the willingness of two universities to continue pursuing the technology to the limit of the phase where new science was likely to be learned. The two years it took to close the research gap, through work at MIT and Penn State and the drug company partnerships, had brought the technology to the point where Edwards could say "[I]t was clear to us that the technology basically worked." The information and trust gap was greatly reduced by the extraordinary reputation Bob Langer enjoyed in both the technical and investment communities.

Thus, even in cases where the conditions are especially favorable—a distinguished inventor who has a professional relationship with a successful and influential investor—the gaps can still be broad and deep.

Trexel, Inc.

In the early 1980s Nam P. Suh, the Ralph E. and Eloise Cross Professor and head of MIT's mechanical engineering department, invented a microcellular foam process for making very strong, lightweight, and inexpensive plastic material. His research was sponsored by a multi-firm subscription to a MIT–Industry Polymer Processing Program. One of the participants, Eastman Kodak, asked if he could find a way to reduce the consumption of plastics in the firm's photographic products.[7] (Eastman later abandoned the project because they could not find an acceptable continuous process that met the performance requirements.) Professor Suh's invention, which required precisely controlled thermodynamic reactions in a thermoplastic raw material, created very evenly distributed and equal-sized bubbles in the plastic, retaining material strength while using less raw material. His technique involved dissolving nitrogen and carbon dioxide gases in the plastic, heating the material under carefully controlled pressure and temperature until the gases created millions of uniform bubbles. In some cases 90 percent of the strength of the solid plastic could be retained while saving 50 percent of the raw material cost.

MIT filed patents on Suh's inventions, which issued in 1983. A decade later Suh founded a company called MuCell (later renamed Trexel) to exploit his ideas commercially. By 1995 his technology had matured enough to attract a high level of attention from customers. It was time to look for capital to accelerate the pace of commercialization. Alex d'Arbeloff, a noted entrepreneur and "angel," was at the time chairman of the MIT visiting committee to the mechanical engineering department. He admired Suh's research and organized a venture investment group that purchased 30 percent of Trexel for $2.2 million.

What had happened in the thirteen years from Suh's invention to d'Arbeloff's investment? Professor Suh's own research continued to explore a wide variety of academically interesting materials and processes. In 1984 he took leave from MIT to head the Engineering Directorate of the National Science Foundation. On his return to MIT in 1988, he received support from a Japanese company interested in his thermoplastic material project. He then recruited some additional firms into a Microcellular Plastics Consortium, and he also received a research grant from the NSF. A few years later he dissolved the consortium, partly because of difficulties over intellectual property rights. The two major technical obstacles were the need to understand how the process could be scaled up to high-volume, very-low-cost production, and how it might need to be adapted to the particular product being fabricated using the MIT process.

Most plastics are fabricated by injection molding. Every product has its own special requirements, suited to the molding machines and the requirements of its use in a final product. Thus it was not sufficient to show the superior material properties that could be obtained in a sample from the test lab; every product had to be developed in partnership with an industrial customer. For this reason Trexel had a dozen licensees who were struggling to include it in their processes.

Trexel is really not a product company; it sells a process. "What I've learned," Trexel CEO David Bernstein told a Harvard-MIT workshop in 1999, "is that it's never a product until it's a product in that particular customer's process, under his particular set of expectations. So we actually take a fairly hard line about how far we're willing to go to prove anything to people, since we're not a product development company per se, we're really moving technology in. We know we'll never get to the end of it. The longer it's ours, the longer it will take to get to the end of it."

Professor Suh is still active as an advisor to the company, but the decade since he made his invention has seen a transformation in the nature of the technical problems facing its commercialization. The technical research and the skills required are far different in character from the work Suh did in his laboratory. Today it is focused on supporting the business model that is most promising, given the understanding of the market gained during the ten years. In the spring of 2000, "MuCell," the process's trade name, attracted great attention at the National Plastics Exhibition in Chicago. Three plastics manufacturers produced MuCell parts at the show, and there were over 2,000 inquiries to Trexel and the three manufacturers.[8]

The conditions surrounding the founding of Trexel were unusually favorable. Alex d'Arbeloff said he was "not the angel investor but rather a finder for his friends," and later, "I am a pessimist about things working. Nam Suh was a good friend and had beautiful samples from his lab. Scale-up was something plastics companies didn't want to take on. Bernstein had worked for Teradyne [which d'Arbeloff founded] and I hired him back." They started out getting customers to fund the project. The first year they made a product, but had little acceptance. They were "trolling" for the right applications. Then they started limiting applications because some were proving too expensive. "Then we funded the project ourselves, now focusing on one process." He thinks they may need to focus even more in the future.

"I am not sure I understand the whole thing about technical risk," d'Arbeloff commented. "You have to work with a technology to know what it is all about. How can you know if a technology you are not using isn't what you need?" So the question is, "How much will you pay to do the work to learn about the technology?"

Risk of What?: Defining Success and Failure

What is known about the attitudes and behavior of those economic actors, faced with opportunities that are at once daunting and attractive, who engage in science-based innovations? The cases we have reviewed suggest that evaluations of risk depend strongly on personal relationships and trust. They also depend on the institutional setting of those who share the risks of new ventures, innovators and investors alike.

The assessment of "risk" depends critically on the definition of success and failure. Clearly, both success and failure are defined in terms of objectives. These objectives may be institutional, personal, or defined at the level of the project. Multiple objectives in a technical project directly imply multiple categories of failure and success.

Institutional Objectives

Consider first institutional objectives. A venture capitalist (VC), for example, may define the success of a technical project exclusively in terms of the expected return on invested capital, regardless of whether the firm abandons one particular set of specifications for another, or even changes its market objective altogether. Success to the VC will thus depend absolutely on the *commercial* viability of the technology in question. In contrast, a government technology project might emphasize specific national security needs, environmental objectives, or even broad benefits to the economy (called "knowledge spillovers") that could ensue from overcoming a particular technological challenge. In the last case—that of projects emphasizing spillover effects—it is possible for the transfer of technical knowledge and generation of positive market dislocations (Schumpeterian "creative destruction") to occur through commercialization. However, knowledge spillovers may also occur through transfer of intellectual property created as result of the project (such as patent citations) or from the knowledge embodied in project researchers as they move forward to new research environments.

Howard Frank, Dean of the Robert H. Smith School of Business at the University of Maryland, describes the methods he used as a program director at the Defense Advanced Research Projects Agency (DARPA):

The level of specification of different technical projects [was] very loose, so that you could define success in many ways. You will never find an unsuccessful DARPA project.

His point is that technical projects with sufficiently ambitious goals almost always produce useful technical knowledge and experience. The same cannot be said of projects supported by investments whose goals are measured in terms of sales in competitive markets.

The university, in turn, is defined by its own unique mission and objectives. Foremost among these are education and the advancement of knowledge—potential objectives for firms and government as well, to be sure, but ones that are at best secondary in those settings. Professor Robert Langer of MIT, out of whose laboratory more than 25 companies (including AIR) have been created, warns of evaluating university research laboratories by metrics similar to those used to evaluate commercial firms. Taking into account his primary responsibilities to his students and to the advancement of science, Langer says of research projects conducted in his laboratory: "I have trouble identifying many failures by my standards as an MIT professor." Thus the extent to which any institution—be it a corporation, a venture capital firm, or a university—is able to achieve its mission is dependent in large part on the harmonization of the objectives of the institution as a whole and those of individuals who make up the institution.

Universities represent a vital source of new technical ideas for firms of all sizes. The ferment of industrial relationships pervades even the most elite academic institutions (Branscomb, Kodama, and Florida 1999). Are universities prepared to undertake research to explore the technologies required to reduce their inventions to commercial practice and prepare them for VC investment? In the two case studies reviewed above, the technologies required to convert original inventions into commercially marketable products were developed in university settings over the course of several years, and VC firms were willing to make major investments only after technical risk was significantly reduced.

Personal Objectives

Harvard Business School professor Josh Lerner emphasizes the importance of harmonizing personal and institutional objectives in the context of new firm formation and funding (Lerner 2000). If a new firm raises equity from outside investors, managers have an incentive to engage in wasteful expenditures because they do not bear their full cost. If instead the firm raises debt, managers have an incentive to decrease levels of risk. Furthermore, even if such problems can be mitigated so that the managers are fully motivated to maximize shareholder value (through harmonizing the objectives of investors and managers), informational asymmetries may complicate efforts to raise capital. The fact that potential investors know less about the inner working of the firms they fund than the managers who run the firms can lead to problems for both groups. For example, managers will have an incentive to offer new shares in the firm only if the stock is overvalued, while concerns over informational asymmetries may lead investors to offer funding under less than favorable conditions. Lerner views venture capitalists as financial intermediaries who are specialized in mitigating problems arising out of the imperfectly harmonized objectives of entrepreneur/managers and potential investors, and thereby minimizing financing constraints that exist on the funding of new firms.

A related but distinct set of competing personal objectives defines the relationship of technology project managers (be they executives in a corporations or CEOs of start-up firms) and the technologists directly responsible for the work of the project team. The information asymmetry is nowhere greater than between the technical expert who champions the project and the financially responsible manager who must commit resources with an inadequate personal mastery of the technical challenges to be faced and the means for their solution. Thus the nature of the communication, and most importantly the degree of trust, between these two parties is probably the most critical element in the management of technical uncertainties.[9] Both parties must accept the reality of these uncertainties and the fact that they can lead to failure. For the innovator they derive from the unpredictability of nature and also from the need to sustain the confidence of the investor. For the investor or business executive the decision about whether to risk the uncertainties must be based on the prior performance of the innovator.

In this situation both parties must face the possibility of failure. But it matters very much how that failure occurs. The technologist has at least two ways to fail. If nature proves unyielding, despite a well-organized and well-managed technical effort and good communications with investors, failure is honorable. If the team is ill-prepared, the effort poorly staffed, knowledge of the state of the art or of the competition is inadequate, and management feels deceived, then failure is dishonorable. Honorable failure will not markedly reduce the technologist's chance of being asked to direct future high-risk research efforts, whereas dishonorable failure has the potential to be career-ending. Similar distinctions between honorable and dishonorable failure exist for both technology managers and entrepreneurs. For technologist and manager alike, long-run personal success will depend far more on cumulative reputation for effectiveness than on the outcome of any single project.

University professors may define their own success or failure in terms of any subset of an exceptionally large and varied set of professional objectives, including (but not limited to) pedagogy, research productivity, administrative effectiveness, aptitude for clinical work, ability to raise funds for research, and public service. Even in the absence of explicitly commercial incentives within the academic setting, there is an inherently entrepreneurial aspect to U.S. academic culture (Etzkowitz 1989). "It is amazing how much being a professor is like running a small business," remarks one faculty member quoted by Henry Etzkowitz (1999). "The system forces you to be very entrepreneurial because everything is driven by financing your group." Another faculty entrepreneur observes: "What is the difference between financing a research group on campus and financing a research group off campus? You have a lot more options off campus, but if you go the federal proposal route, it is really very similar."

This inherent correspondence between academic and entrepreneurial cultures has become significantly reinforced in the past twenty years by both the passage of the Bayh-Dole Act and the dramatic growth of the biotechnology industry, largely as the outcome of successful efforts to create new firms out of university research efforts.[10] Incentive structures in university research laboratories have by both design and necessity become increasingly similar to those found in corporate research laboratories and start-up firms. A current and ongoing concern for university administrators and policy makers alike is ensuring that universities as institutions, and university professors and researchers as individuals, receive their fair share of the direct monetary rewards from their innovative efforts while preserving the particular objectives that distinguish and define the university.[11] Thus the modern research university in the United States sits largely on the scientific side of the research gap, but may in some fields, especially those leading to biomedical and information service innovations, extend its research agenda into the gap in order to benefit from the commercialization of faculty inventions.

Project Objectives

Given the foregoing discussion of the personal and institutional objectives in terms of which success and failure may be defined, we now turn our attention to the objectives of the technical project itself. Long before the market delivers its judgment on the value of a new technology, the technology must pass through a number of stages of development.

Any temporal partition of the innovation process is bound to be arbitrary and imperfect. A distinction that has the benefit of being frequently employed by practitioners (particularly in the life sciences) is that between "proof of principle" and "reduction to practice":

• *Proof of principle* means that a project team has demonstrated its ability, within a research setting, to meet a well-defined technological challenge: to show in a laboratory setting that a model of a commercial product, process, or service can demonstrate the function that, if produced in quantity at low enough cost and high enough reliability, could meet an identified market opportunity. It involves the successful application of basic scientific principles to the solution of a specific problem.[12]

• *Reduction to practice* means that a working model of a product has been developed in the context of well-defined and unchanging specifications, using processes not unlike those that will be required for scaled-up production. Product design and production processes can be defined that have sufficient "windows" for variability to constitute a reliable product made through a high-yield, stable process. In simple English, the technical risk has been reduced enough so that the innovator-entrepreneur can say to managers and investors, "Yes, I can do that, and do it at a cost and on a schedule in which we can all have confidence."

Professor Ron Burback of the Computer Science Department at Stanford University distinguishes the proof of principle phase from the producible prototype stage in software development as follows: "[In the proof of principle phase,] teams work simultaneously on all phases of the problem. The analysis team generates requirements. The design team discusses requirements and feeds back complexity issues to the requirement team and feeds critical implementation tasks to the implementation team. The testing team prepares and develops the testing environment based on the requirements…. One of the goals of this stage is for the teams to convince themselves that a solution can be accomplished." He describes the "prototype" stage as follows: "The requirements and the requirement document are frozen and placed under change-order control. Changes in requirements are still allowed but should be very rare.... One of the goals of this stage is for the team to convince non-team members that the solution can be accomplished" (Burback 1998).

Failure at either of these stages might involve an unexpected technical problem that available skills and knowledge cannot solve. Alternatively, as in the example of superconducting Josephson technology as a possible replacement for silicon transistors (described in the essay by James McGroddy, former chief technical officer of IBM, in this volume), the technology may be said to fail, despite successful proof of principle and reduction to practice, because the pace of progress in the competing and better-established technology is seriously underestimated, or because of some other event, exogenous to the project itself, that alters the market environment in an unacceptable way—the appearance of a formidable competitor, a change in patterns of use or demand, new government regulations, and so on.

While there is value to clearly defining project success and failure as a prerequisite to evaluating risks, some technical managers in private firms may choose to leave the question of success or failure in suspension for a considerable period of time. David Lewis (2000) describes the strategy of burying a technology failure in "a shallow grave." A manager may stop the flow of funds to a project whose progress is blocked by an unresolvable technical difficulty, but retain both the technical knowledge and the awareness of market potential, pending a new idea that would justify resurrecting the project. Lewis further observes that the ability to quantify risk is dependent on how far the project is from the market: "The more that is known and understood about the total [market] area, the higher the probability of correctly assessing and dealing with the specific issue of technical risk. This is especially true during the market requirements phase."

Larry Jarrett, a director of the Industrial Research Institute and formerly vice president of OrganoSilicones R&D of Witco Corporation, further observes that because failure is an outcome of the uncertainties associated with risk taking, it is to be expected in an innovative organization. Furthermore, a persistent team can often turn a technical "failure" (in terms of original objectives) into an ex post market success. (This phenomenon is facetiously described in one company as, "If you can't fix it, feature it.")[13] Jarrett and others note that there exist many cases in which the final success is not the use originally intended. For established firms, eventual success may result from residual technology values that are later used in as-yet-unforeseen markets (such as the 3-M Post-it, the product of a "failed" adhesive), or from what is learned about a market and its business during the failed project. However, as Steve Kent of GTE-BBN Corporation observes, the extent to which failures are "useful" in this sense depends on firm size. Start-up companies whose big projects fail often simply go out of business, in which case technology and business learning is preserved and transferred only by former employees who go to work elsewhere; big companies may be able to place failures into the portfolio for the future.[14]

Aligning Objectives, Creating Options

We started this chapter by emphasizing the role of extraordinary profits in drawing forth the effort required to turn inventions into innovations. In the words of Schumpeter (1942: 73–74), "Spectacular prizes much greater than would have been necessary to call forth the particular effort are thrown to a small minority of winners, thus propelling much more efficaciously than a more equal and 'just' distribution would, the activity of that large majority of businessmen who receive very modest compensation or nothing or less than nothing." The rewards for the few winners must in some sense compensate all those who receive almost nothing, or less than nothing, beyond what they could have earned in another activity. Of course, particular opportunities for extraordinary profits are "transient"—hundred dollar bills don't stay on the sidewalk for long. Yet the vitality of the innovation system over time depends at least as much on the continued availability of opportunities for rewards from innovation ("demand pull" in the jargon) as it does on the continued availability of technological advances that can be converted into product innovations ("supply push").

Invention and market opportunities are both necessary conditions for innovation, but they are not sufficient. Potential rewards of any magnitude may seem negligible if expected far enough into the future, or if uncertain enough. But that is not all. Even when science is proven and market opportunities are real, effort toward technology-based innovation must bridge a funding gap (between academic and commercial support), a research gap (between research judgments made on "interestingness" criteria and those made based on a market potential criterion), and a trust/information gap (between the technologist and managers/investors). Bridging these three gaps requires aligning the potentially divergent objectives of the individuals involved, the supporting institutions, and the project itself—creating not only a common perception of opportunities, but also a shared definition of risks and rewards. The paper by George Hartmann and Mark Myers that follows this chapter details the manner in which risks and rewards are defined, quantified, and analyzed in the context of the Xerox innovation system.

Notes

1. These include economies of scale (see e.g. Bain 1956 and Schmalensee 1981); sunk costs such as R&D and/or advertising intensity (see e.g. Dixit 1981 and Sutton 1991); informational impediments to imitation (see e.g. Lippman and Rumelt 1982, and Mansfield 1985); and extent of first-mover advantages, such as those due to consumer switching costs (see e.g. Schmalensee 1982), network externalities (see e.g. Arthur 1989) and/or learning by doing (see e.g. Smiley and Ravid 1983).

2. In contrast, business schools devote a great deal of effort to identifying the "secrets" behind the extraordinary success stories of such exceptional companies as IBM, Intel, Amazon.com—even Microsoft.

3. While this statement is self-evident today, it was not so even 60 years ago; Schumpeter (1942) devotes a substantial portion of a chapter titled "The Vanishing of Investment Opportunities" to rejecting the proposition that the closing of geographical (or colonial) frontiers implies an era of diminishing economic opportunities: "It is gratuitous to assume not only that the 'closing of the frontier' will cause a vacuum, but also that whatever steps into the vacant space must necessarily be less important in any of the senses we may choose to give to that word. The conquest of the air may well be more important than the conquest of India was—we must not confuse geographical frontiers with economic ones."

4. This rather dramatic description of the gap between invention and innovation has an obscure origin, but has been popularized by Ehlers (1998).

5. The uncertainty of intellectual property protection for the newly developed innovation represents a fourth critical challenge for early-stage, technology-based innovation. This uncertainty is, of course, not resolved when a patent is granted; as Lanjouw and Shankerman (1997) find in their study of trends in patent litigation, disputes are particularly frequent in new technology areas.

6. David Edwards, private communication to Michael Roberts, 24 July 2000.

7. This case illustrates one source of research funding that might go beyond basic academic research and begin to address "gap" technologies—sponsorship by a possible ultimate customer of the innovation. This is not unusual in the pharmaceutical industry, nor is it unusual for polytechnic institutions like MIT.

8. Professor Suh notes that MuCell increases the productivity of injection molding machines by as much as 50%, decreases the molding pressure by an order of magnitude, and makes parts that are strong, light, and stable.

9. In Chapter IV we will see that for this reason the middle-sized, technology-specialized firm may have intrinsic advantages. The individuals who produce the innovative ideas and reduce them to practice may also have profit-and loss-responsibility in the firm, dramatically reducing the information and trust asymmetries.

10. Mowery et al. (1999) analyze the effects of the Bayh-Dole Act in detail.

11. Etzkowitz (1999) describes the strong entrepreneurial culture at Stanford and MIT, and the emergence of such a culture at other leading research universities. Thursby and Thursby (2000) report that technology licensing activity at a sample of large research universities increased at a rate of 8% a year from 1994 to1997. They find, however, little evidence to reinforce concerns that faculty have redirected their research toward commercial applications. Instead they find that the recent growth in university licensing of technologies is "due primarily to an increased willingness of faculty and administrators to license and increased business reliance on external R&D rather than a shift in faculty research toward work with greater commercial possibilities."

12. In the life sciences, "proof of principle" is achieved "when a compound has shown the desired activity *in vitro* that supports a hypothesis or concept for use of compounds." (This definition is taken from Karo Bio AB <www.karobio.se>, a drug discovery company.)

13. A current example is the yogurt advertisement for "Dannon Fruit on the Bottom." When fruit is added to yogurt it sinks to the bottom of the container and is not visible to the consumer, a disadvantage that was simply incorporated into the name of the product.

14. In the 1960s the IBM "Stretch" supercomputer was regarded as a failure, but the technology it pioneered appeared in the System 360, the most successful computer project in the industry's history. Again in 1972 IBM undertook a huge program to change both the architecture and the technology in its main frame series. This $500 million development program, called Future System, was

scrapped, but the architecture showed up in the very successful AS 400, and much of the technology appeared in the evolving main frame machines. (See Watson 2000.)

Technical Risk, Product Specifications, and Market Risk

George C. Hartmann and Mark B. Myers

Xerox is a multinational corporation with $19.4 billion annual revenues. In addition, Fuji Xerox, jointly owned by Xerox and Fuji Photo Film Co., Ltd., has annual revenues of $6.8 billion, giving the company revenues on a worldwide basis of $26.2 billion. Fuji Xerox manufactures and distributes products in Japan and the Pacific Rim. Xerox Corporation offers products and services related to documents and associated information technologies. An ongoing challenge is creation of new products to refresh the product line as well as to grow revenue, requiring the generation of more than $3 billion additional revenue each year. To accomplish this, Xerox spends approximately 6% of revenue on research, development, and engineering (RD&E) annually, and uses a disciplined innovation process and product delivery system. About four-fifths of the RD&E budget is invested in product engineering and manufacturing, the remaining one-fifth is invested in research and advanced technology development.

The product development and time-to-market process, illustrated in Figure 1, includes research, technology development, and product development activities, each of which drives risk down. Research is an on-going activity that spawns ideas, inventions, and new technologies that must be reduced to practice. If promising, a new technology must then be developed, often concurrently with other sub-systems, for an envisioned market application. An objective of the technology development activity, illustrated by the middle box in Figure 1, is to demonstrate the performance potential of the technology and address robustness and manufacturing

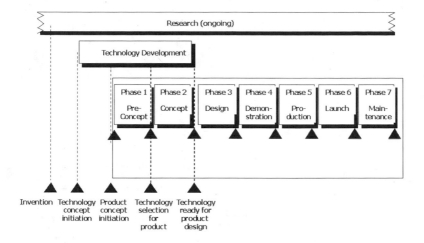

Figure 1 Product development and time-to-market process.

issues to reduce technology risk. A second objective is to refine the customer requirements to reduce market risk and to evolve specifications.

The six boxes labeled Phase 1 to Phase 6 in the lower part of Figure 1 illustrate the product development process, which delivers final product specifications, product design, factory design and product manufacture, and product launch infrastructure. Technology development may occur concurrently in all three types of activities. Typically, decisions about the degree of concurrency depend on the objectives of the product program, and how much risk the product chief engineer is willing to accept. In many situations, it is best to demonstrate technology feasibility before committing to an expensive and time-sensitive product development effort. At any one time, on the order of 300 projects may be underway in various stages of the pipeline, from research to product launch. Over 90 products are launched annually.

A key mission of the Xerox Research and Technology (XRT) organization is to create options in the form of technology opportunities matched to markets, consistent with the strategic direction of the corporation. A second mission is to reduce the technical and market risk inherent in these new technology opportunities. The market risk is strongly linked to the technology through the

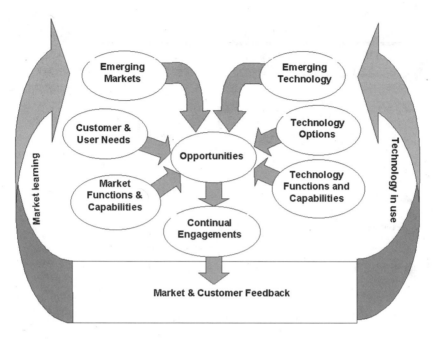

Figure 2 Iterative innovation for creation of new business value.

customer requirements, which may be explicitly known, or stated as a working assumption in the early phases.

As technology development proceeds, eventually these requirements must be restated in technical terms in the form of a specification, with target performance goals and a specified product launch date. The process of refining the technology capabilities and the customer requirements, which eventually evolve into a specification, is iterative, as depicted in Figure 2 (Myers 1996). We often use Quality Function Deployment (QFD), a powerful technique for evolving and refining the specification. The formalism of QFD emphasizes the intimate linkage between the technology characteristics and market requirements (Akao 1990).

Elements of Risk

The importance of describing and managing the market and technical risks of emergent technologies has been emphasized in books dealing with management of technology, and techniques for

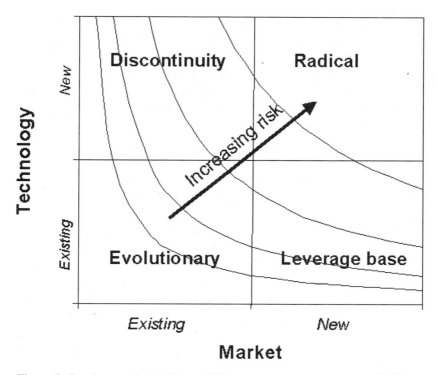

Figure 3 Quadrants of risk. The solid lines represent constant overall risk.

risk quantification are discussed there (Roussel, Saad, and Erickson 1991, Smith and Reinertsen 1998, McGrath, Anthony, and Shapiro 1992). Investments in research and technology have to be placed into a portfolio of risk, assessed in terms of markets and technology. As Figure 3 shows, one can distinguish four quadrants according to the degree of market and technology risk:

• *Evolutionary (existing markets, existing technology):* lowest risk, but possibly limited economic potential.

• *Leverage base (new markets, existing technology):* somewhat higher risk. For a global company, opportunities of this type tend to be geographical.

• *Discontinuities (existing markets, new technology):* somewhat higher risk. This case refers to technology substitution, a familiar situation.

• *Radical (new markets, new technology):* highest risk. If the market is large, this may offer the greatest opportunity.

Several examples illustrate these risk categories. The Xerox 8010 information system and 6085 professional workstation with ViewPoint icons and windowing software is an example of the *radical* quadrant. In 1981, this was a brand-new technology in an untried market. Competitive risk was low due to first-mover advantages, but intellectual property protection was weak. The market was not prepared to use the product, and no complementary industry existed. Customers had limited choices; nevertheless they could choose from three versions: network, remote, and standalone. The business plan was not clear. Xerox had the world's best computer scientists on the project, so the technical competency was high. But customer requirements were not well known, and product specifications were risky. Although several document-processing applications were offered, in hindsight, the "killer application" turned out to be the Lotus 1-2-3 spreadsheet that went out with the IBM personal computer. Xerox itself became a major user of the 6085, with tens of thousands of units installed throughout the company, but the product had limited commercial success, and it was later abandoned.

Hewlett Packard's thermal ink-jet printing provides examples in two quadrants. Initially, HP launched this new technology into an existing market of pen plotters and dot-matrix printing: a technology displacement without high market risk. This fits in the *discontinuity* quadrant. After perfecting and refining the technology, HP moved into new markets of desktop printing and, more recently, into home photo-printing (examples of the *leveraged base* quadrant).

Xerox's Liveboard provides another example of the *radical* quadrant, with a new technology in a new market. Liveboard was a computationally active whiteboard with remote communications capabilities using Unix. This was launched into a new market before working out a sound business model, in the belief that a market "had to be out there." Product price was high, and opportunities to develop manufacturing economies of scale were limited. Eventually Microsoft Windows was substituted for Unix because customers wanted compatibility with existing systems, which took away some proprietary technology opportunities. Following a short exploratory market probe, the product was withdrawn.

Quantification of Risk—An Example

Risk comes in many forms, often difficult to enumerate, much less quantify. Our discussion is limited to the nature of technologies undertaken by Xerox: technologies that involve electromechanical systems, electronics, digital image processing, control systems, document management tools, and information management tools. Our approach is to identify major contributors to technology and market risk. For each contributing element, an anchored scale is constructed with a score that provides an approximate measure of the probability of success. Six contributors to risk are identified: three each for technology risk and market risk. Components of technology risk include the risk of being able to resolve any remaining technical problems adequately, the risk of having available the necessary competencies and complementary technologies required for commercialization, and the risk of achieving the technical specifications necessary to meet customer expectations. Components of market risk include the risk of having value chain elements (such as engineering, manufacturing, marketing, distribution, and sales) available for delivery, the risk that the product will provide vectors of differentiation sufficient to distinguish it from competitive offerings, and the risk that the proposed business model will be successful in the market.

Technology Risk

Three types of technology risk are quantified in Table 1 and described below.

Technical Risk. Technical risk refers to the set of technical problems associated with a new or emerging technology. The characterization of technical risk in physical systems (as opposed to software) has been discussed elsewhere (Hartmann and Lakatos 1998: 32); we summarize it here. With a new or emerging technology, many types of "technology problems" will be encountered. "Technology problems" can arise from application of a new process, material, or subsystem before fully understanding the parameters that control performance, cost, safe operating latitudes, or failure modes. They can occur if a previously commercialized technology is extended

Table 1 Technology Risk Quantification Model

Technology Risk Elements

Technical risk (P_1)	Availability of competencies & complementary technologies required to deliver the technology (P_2)	Specification achieveability (P_3)	Probability of success (for each element)
Incremental extension of existing in-house technology	Technology and advanced development competencies available, complementary technologies exist	Modest extension of existing specifications & performance requirements	0.9
Incremental extension of existing outside technology	Technology competency not available, advanced development competency and complementary technologies available	Major extension of specifications/ performance	0.7
New technology, feasibility demonstrated	Technology competency and complementary technologies available, advanced development competency not available	New specification in a new performance domain	0.5
New technology, feasibility not demonstrated	Technology or advanced development competencies available elsewhere, complementary technologies not available	Some specifications unknown or unknowable	0.3
New invention, not reduced to practice	Neither technology & advanced development competencies nor complementary technologies available	No specification known	0.1

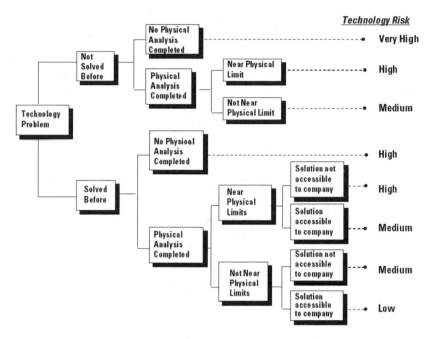

Figure 4 Algorithm for assigning technical risk in physical systems.

outside the known domains of the pertinent design rules. They can also occur from unexpected interactions arising from a new or unique combination of subsystems or components. An example is the requirement for much more precise motion quality when digital imaging subsystems are substituted into hardware that was previously based on analog technology.

Periodically during the technology development process, "technology reviews" should be conducted in which technology champions and a peer group of subject-matter experts participate. These reviews enable a list of anticipated or known technology problems to be generated and tracked over time. Each technology problem can be rated using a uniform method, such as the "technical risk" algorithm shown in Figure 4. This information can be aggregated to create a risk profile for the new technology that can be followed over time, and to position the new technology on the scale in Table 1.

As technologies move from the research bench to product development, there is an inherent tension between the technology champions and the product chief engineer. The technologist creates new concepts, new surprises, and new risks. He or she is optimistic, is successful if his or her ideas are adopted, and may overstate the merits. The chief engineer, on the other hand, tries to solve problems, avoid surprises, and minimize risk; he or she is successful if the product meets the specification on schedule, irrespective of the technology used. The technical risk approach outlined here is intended to provide a framework for managing this inherent tension, to help identify the risk as soon as possible so that appropriate measures can be taken. As Richard Feynman said during the investigation of the Challenger disaster, "for a successful technology, reality must take precedence over public relations, for Nature cannot be fooled" (Feynman 1989: 237).

Availability of competencies and complementary technologies required. Development of a new technology may require new technical skills, tools, and processes, or may require access to skills and tools already committed to other technology and product development efforts. Complementary technologies may be required to work in concert with the new technology, but may not be ready or implemented. In some instances, a critical resource is the technical know-how necessary to integrate the new technology into an existing system. Systems integration and systems engineering skills are usually in high demand and often not available. If the critical skills must be acquired outside the corporation, for example through a development contract, appropriate interfaces and partnerships must be devised. If the required skills simply do not exist, they must be developed concurrently with technology and product development, which introduces additional risk. Table 1 provides a guide for judging these dimensions of risk.

Specification achieveability. As new technology moves toward product, performance must eventually be quantified and characterized in terms of the targeted product specification. What we are referring to here is not the risk that the target specification has been properly selected based on the customer need and market requirements, but the risk that the technology performance is insufficient to meet the target specification. Examples include the possibility of shortfalls in parameters related to quality, speed, reliability, and cost. These problems are difficult to nail down until the product specification and design intent have been identified. Moreover, the assessment of this risk factor is often entangled with the technical risk above, depending on the newness of the envisioned product concept.

Market Risk

The market risk is separated into three factors, described below and listed in Table 2.

Availability of value chain elements. Market success of a new technology requires many things to fall in place, in addition to the technology. For example, the corporation needs to have the engagement of product engineering, manufacturing, marketing, distribution, and sales organizations. For a new technology, especially in a product offering in a new market, many of these elements may not be in place, or if they are, may not be prepared to deal with the new product. Consequently this area represents a significant risk. Table 2 offers a guide for this dimension of risk.

Product vector of differentiation. New products may offer some compelling combination of product functions, features, or economics to differentiate them from existing products. Some of these product capabilities may be enabled by the new technology. There are several risks. For example, when the product specifications were created, product planning may have underestimated how rapidly competition would raise the bar, and in the worst case, the product would offer capability at launch less than competitive offerings. More likely, product planning would respond before product launch by modifying the target specification during product development. "Specification creep" can push the technology into difficult performance regimes, increasing the risk and/or delaying the schedule. In the meantime, the competition advances again. Another risk is that the customer does not perceive the performance or feature enabled by the technology as an advantage. More than one technologist has been disappointed when customers simply did not care about the marvels of the technology embedded in the product.

Market acceptance. In some instances, the product may flow into a market in which the corporation is active, and where it has a business model, understands the customers, competition, and market dynamics. Products introduced into new markets offer higher risk; for example, less may be known about the customers.

Table 2 Market Risk Quantification Model

Market Risk Elements

Availability of value chain elements (P_4)	Product vector of differentiation (P_5)	Market acceptance and business model (P_6)	Probability of success (for each element)
Value chain is available within the company	Product is best in class in all attributes	Company is currently in the market	0.9
Major elements of company's value chain must be developed	Product is best in some attributes, but not all	Company has contact with customers, but is not in the market	0.7
Company value chain is broken, many elements not available	Product offers advantages in one or two attributes	Company is active in a closely related market	0.5
No value chain elements exist within the company	Product has same profile as competitors	Market exists, but only as a "niche," business model not established	0.3
Critical value chain elements do not exist anywhere	Product offers advantage in one or two attributes, but is worse in all others	Market and business model does not exist	0.1

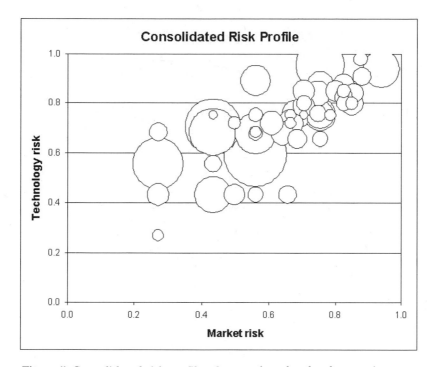

Figure 5 Consolidated risk profile of research and technology projects.

In some instances, a business model may simply not exist, and no one has any idea of the potential size of the market. Table 2 suggests a method of quantifying this risk.

Application

All research and technology activities in Xerox Research & Technology were scored by subject domain experts, using the scales in Tables 1 and 2. Fifty-five technologies were scored. The scores were consolidated using:

Technology risk = $1 - (P_1 \cdot P_2 \cdot P_3)$

Market risk = $1 - (P_4 \cdot P_5 \cdot P_6)$

The consolidated scores are displayed in Figure 5, in which the bubble area is proportional to the investment. A corresponding chart, not shown here, can be made in which the bubble area is

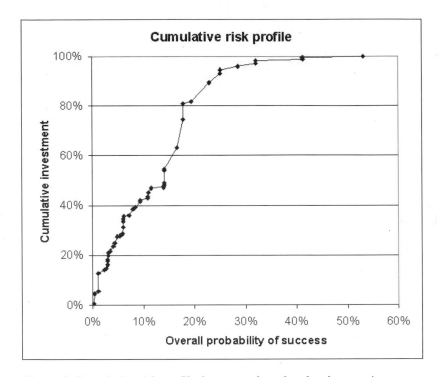

Figure 6 Cumulative risk profile for research and technology projects.

proportional to the estimated market value of each technology project.

The overall probability of success for each technology project can be estimated:

Overall probability of success = $P_1 \cdot P_2 \cdot P_3 \cdot P_4 \cdot P_5 \cdot P_6$

This information can be summarized as shown in Figure 6, which illustrates the cumulative investment plotted against the overall probability of success. This plot shows the overall risk profile of the research and technology investment. Projects with the smallest investments tend to have small probabilities of success, and vice versa, illustrated by the density of points on different regions of the curve. Once again, a corresponding chart can be made in which the cumulative market value of each project is plotted as a function of the overall probability of success.

The four charts just described (two of which are shown in Figures 5 and 6) provide information useful for understanding the risks and potential rewards of the research and technology investment stream.

This information and the techniques described by Roussel, Saad, and Erickson can be used to help manage the risk (Roussel, Saad, and Erickson, 1991). The technology and product decision makers must work together continuously to drive the risk down, and track progress in risk reduction over time.

Concluding Remarks

As others have pointed out, there are inherent difficulties with risk analysis. Admittedly it is impossible to know if all the risks have been identified, or whether an adequate measure of each identified risk has been constructed. Another aspect is that management can become too comfortable and forget the "real" risk, which includes things as yet unknown. We advocate a balance between a purely analytic approach and an intuitive one, and endorse an approach that explicitly deals with the risk arising from the interplay between technology and market.

II

Defining Risks and Rewards

[Risk] is a statistical term, and therefore, I think, very inapplicable to single projects.... When you go to jump across the chasm, you either make it or you don't.
—James McGroddy

Properly speaking, the ability to describe the "risk" of failure inherent in a technical project implies some prior experience. It is not possible, for example, to talk meaningfully about a given project having a "10 percent probability of success" in the absence of some accumulated prior experience (such as a sample of similar projects of which nine in ten were failures). To the extent that a technical team is attempting to overcome a truly novel challenge, it may more properly be said to be facing uncertainty rather than risk.[1] The distinction is more than academic. If the probabilities of failure can be reliably calculated, conditional on observable facts, risks can be easily managed. If technical projects were mere spins of the roulette wheel, a few dozen trips to the table would suffice to yield a payoff for any given "number" chosen at random.[2] Such is not, however, typically the case with early-stage, high-risk technical projects.[3]

Uncertainty describes the absence of sufficient information to predict the outcome of a project. Mark Myers, in the foregoing essay, observes that "uncertainty [provides the motivation] to create options.... Uncertainty and risk are quite different. Risk offers great harm; uncertainty offers great opportunity. We see ourselves refining that uncertainty so that the risks are essentially removed." Whereas risk is a quantification of potential failure, uncertainty is the context for the opportunities that drive innovation from the outset. Returning to our original analogy: Uncertainty is the boundary between an action taken and an action not taken, while risk represents the prospect that the action taken will yield a less than desirable outcome.

As pointed out by Larry Jarrett of Witco Corporation, the quantification of technical risk is as much an art as it is a science:

The elements of technical risk are not easily characterized, since real technical risk involves a forecast of how science will pan out when real people conduct experimentation, interpret results, and apply them in real situations. The elements of technical risk are chaotic, in that they are dependent on people and environment, as well as the laws of science (some of which are known, and some of which are unknown at any point in time). And elements of technical risk are not independent of one another: actions to understand and mitigate risk are interrelated through the laws of science, patterns of rational processes, and the personalities of people involved. Risk can be characterized as a probability of success, but it is always a probability given a set of premises, an expected environment, and a pattern of response with a correlated expectation of success.

Jarrett goes on to note, though, that there are many well-established methodologies for assessing technical risk, including anchored scales and probabilistic methods.[4] In the anchored scales approach, elements of technical risk are scored according to their eventual beneficial or adverse impact on project success. To provide consistency across a portfolio of projects, the scales for these scores are "anchored" by describing levels of risk as unambiguously as possible. Often the project manager will undertake a two-part appraisal, assessing first the probability of technical success (based on a comparison of the firm's capabilities with the particulars of the technical challenge at hand), and second the probability of commercial success (assuming that technical success is assured). The overall probability of success for a project is then approximated as the product of these two probabilities. This overall success probability of success can be associated with a percentage scale either subjectively (by a consensus of experienced practitioners), or objectively (by means of comparison with success rates of past projects).[5]

An alternative approach—which appears on this surface to be more rigorous—is to model explicitly the whole process of research, development, and commercialization. The stages are represented via a process map, which then becomes a model system. Blocks represent key transformations, and connections between the blocks represent physical flows, knowledge flows, or both. The output from a block is modeled as the probability distribution of outcomes related to the inputs (also probabilistic) to the block. When the blocks are connected in a computer program, the system is complete. Many simulated project "histories" can be computed. The totality of these simulated histories generate an overall probability distribution of outcomes (conditional on the assumed probability used as inputs at each stage of the simulations). The result is a forecast probability distribution of the degree of success that can be expected. The apparent rigor of such a detailed modeling approach is, however, subverted by the extreme subjectivity of the probability distributions that must be constructed at each juncture in the model system, and by the simplifications needed to construct such a process map in the first place.

In their essay George Hartmann and Mark Myers describe in some detail the methods used at Xerox Corp. to quantify technical risk.[6] Even when intrinsic uncertainties overwhelm such efforts to quantify risks, however, the process of identifying their sources can greatly aid management in dealing systematically with risks.

The difficulty of quantifying the uncertainties associated with early-stage technical projects is only one of the conceptual difficulties with a statistically based definition of technical "risk." A second difficulty is that technical projects tend to have binary outcomes: Projects are either terminated when they encounter severe obstacles or are supported all the way to market introduction (perhaps with modifications in both technology and market objective). As James McGroddy observes:

[Risk] is a statistical term, and therefore, I think, very inapplicable to single projects.... When you go to jump across the chasm, you either make it or you don't. It's not a continuous thing. And I think what risk management is about is identifying the points at which you can fall in the chasm, focusing your energy and focusing the rate at which you invest, consistent with the view that you've got to jump across this Grand Canyon on your motorcycle.

McGroddy observes that risk is the price of doing something that appears to be worthwhile. Risk is not desirable in itself, nor is risk necessarily something to be minimized. An important attribute of risk-taking is that a project is deliberately undertaken because the rewards, multiplied by the (presumably known or estimable) probability of achieving those rewards, exceed the cost of taking the risk. After all, McGroddy notes, "Killing the project minimizes risk but it also eliminates reward."

Modeling Innovation and Risk and Options

If risk is hard to quantify, can the stages in the innovation process at least be modeled in such a way as to illustrate the different ways in which risk arises in a high-tech innovation?

David Lewis of Lord Corp. describes the ways in which technical risk is manifest across three stages in the product development process: (i) basic invention/concept; (ii) achievement of market requirements; and (iii) robust commercialization. The first of these stages describes the type of work undertaken in a corporate or (increasingly) university research laboratory. This stage ends with a laboratory demonstration of phenomena that, if commercialized, might offer attractive business opportunities. The second stage begins when a firm takes up the concept and begins to reduce it to practice—that is, to demonstrate the designs and processes necessary to achieve the assumed requirements of the market that make up the business case. The third phase, robust commercialization, encompasses the firm's response to a well-understood market opportunity with a full product line at competitive costs and quality. Note that these three stages are not intended to imply a linear model of innovation. Research activity in the first stage, for example, may be triggered by a "stage three" market discontinuity that signals potential opportunity. Reduction to practice (stage two) requires the satisfaction of technical specifications, regardless of how those specifications arose.

Lewis's model is consistent with the model advanced by Peck and Scherer (1962) and summarized in Scherer (1999).[7] Scherer observes to begin with that "in an R&D project, uncertainties decline as spending accelerates." Figure II-1 illustrates the relative rate of decline of uncertainty. The product will pass through a technical

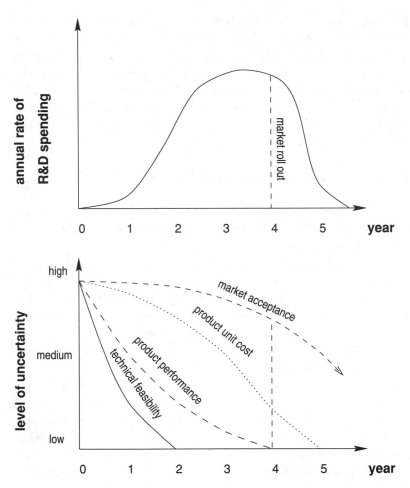

Figure II-1 Relationship between R&D project spending and changes in outcome uncertainty. Source: Scherer (1999: 66), adapted from Peck and Scherer (1962: 313).

feasibility phase, a development phase, an introduction phase, and a market acceptance phase. Uncertainties concerning technical feasibility are resolved much earlier than those concerning cost and market acceptance. As risk falls, moving down on the axis, the firm accelerates spending. If the technical feasibility phase raises unexpected difficulties, the firm may choose not to accelerate spending.

In the event of technical difficulties that could not be foreseen, a project can be stopped at a time when only a fraction of the planned expense has been committed. This fact reduces the barrier that technical dimensions of risk otherwise pose.[8] The largest elements of business risk are referred to collectively as market risks: uncertainties attributable to competitors and consumer responses and by all the other factors that together determine business outcomes. Scherer hypothesizes that:

The cheapest thing and the most important thing to do first is to demonstrate that the technology actually works in an environment that looks something like the manufacturing environment. Until you've done that, it's pretty hard to demonstrate that the product function is what the conceiver of this program had in mind, and certainly to get some quantitative information about likely unit cost of production, ... even though the market risk is surely the biggest ... risk that one faces.

Weighing Technical Risk and Market Risk

The general consensus among practitioners at the two Harvard-MIT workshops was that technical risks are, in general, more manageable than other sources of risk, in the sense that the research process for dealing with them is understood. Venture capital investors such as David Morgenthaler took the view that "Many of the good venture capital firms that we know ... say that they would rather take a technical risk than a market risk. I think that's partly because we can evaluate technical risk better. To launch a fascinating technology out into a very uncertain market is an interesting experience and it's usually cost me a good deal of money." Richard Burnes of Charles River Ventures agreed: "We love technical risk. When we find a team that comes in where we see [technical] risk, typically we know where to get the people who can execute on that risk." Myers supported this view by noting that technical risks are much more accessible to deterministic tools than are some of the market risks at an early stage in a new product innovation.

In the Xerox innovation model described by Hartmann and Myers in the preceding essay, the invention phase (what Lewis refers to as the basic invention/concept stage) is seen as located in Corporate Research. The next stage, that of technology development, includes the transfer of the invention to the product organization and selection of the technology required for the project and for product design. The following stages, including post-technology development, demonstrate, produce, launch, and maintain the product. Like others in the workshop, Hartmann observes that "the process of refining the technology capabilities and customer requirements, which eventually evolve into a specification, is iterative ... and has a virtuous learning nature to it." As Hartmann and Myers note, decision-making within the Xerox Research organization at every stage in the technology development process is guided by two closely related missions: (1) "to create options in the form of technology opportunities matched to markets, consistent with the strategic direction of the corporation"; and (2) "to reduce the technical and market risk inherent in these new technology opportunities."[9] Creating options means taking actions in the present that generate new options in the future. The options approach to managing technical risk emphasizes the value of information gathered over time either by taking an action or by waiting.[10]

Interdependence of Technical and Market Uncertainties

Is it really possible to separate technical uncertainty from market uncertainty? In a radical technical innovation, can one expect to define product and process specifications, then engage in research that is sufficient to reduce technical uncertainties to an acceptable level? Larry Jarrett observes that "risk is defined ... with respect to a specification, and you don't know what the specification is—or what it should have been—when you begin."

Specifications are the link between technical challenges and the market. Specifications may be unstable for several reasons. In the most extreme situation, new information about the requirements of the customer may change, or may be revealed, during the execution of the product program. If the available technology cannot adapt to this change, the project may die (or be placed in what Lewis calls "a shallow grave"), awaiting someone in the firm to make a discovery or invention that addresses the new requirement.

In Chapter IV we quote David Lewis's description of one case in which this happened. As he describes it, "This is an example of a case where technical risk was considered and understood at project

> Production Specifications: Linking Technical Risk and Market Risk in Radical Innovations (Three Cases)
>
> • *The Xerox 8010 information system and 6085 professional workstation with ViewPoint icons and windowing software:* In 1981, the Xerox 8010 information system and 6085 workstation represented brand-new technology in an untried market. Competitive risk was low due to first-mover advantages, and the technical competency of the team was very high. However, intellectual property protection was weak, customer requirements were not well known, and no complementary industry existed. Several document-processing applications were offered, but the "killer application" turned out to be the Lotus 1-2-3 spreadsheet that went out with the IBM personal computer. The product had limited commercial success, and was later abandoned.
>
> • *Hewlett Packard thermal inkjet printing:* Initially, HP launched this new technology into an existing market of pen plotters and dot-matrix printing: a technology displacement without high market risk. After perfecting and refining the technology, HP moved into new markets of desktop printing and, more recently, into home photo-printing (examples of the leveraged base quadrant).
>
> • *The Xerox Liveboard.* Liveboard was a computationally active whiteboard with remote communications capabilities using Unix. Confidence in the technological quality of the product fed a belief that a market "had to be out there." Product price was high, business model unclear. Eventually Microsoft Windows was substituted for Unix because customers wanted compatibility with existing systems. This took away some proprietary technology opportunities. Following a short exploratory market probe, the product was withdrawn.
>
> (Abstracted from Hartmann and Myers, this volume)

inception, but where technical risk changed drastically with changing understanding of market requirements."

More commonly, the specifications change when the performance of the technology is different from what was assumed at the beginning of the project. Those differences require an adjustment in the specifications, which in turn requires that market estimates be adjusted, which in turn may suggest a further adjustment in product specifications. Why are product specifications not predictable at the time of the first proof of concept of the idea when a working prototype is built? The technical demands on a product intended for production and sale are very different from those required for a laboratory demonstration. Often the materials from which the product is made must be chosen for their manufacturability. Process technologies for use in the factory will affect product performance as well. Variations in all the parameters of the materials properties and production processes must be tolerable. These so-called process windows determine production yields and thus costs and usually reliability as well. Every refinement in the technology has its effect on performance and cost.

Sometimes the result of this reduction-to-practice research changes the market opportunity dramatically. Nanophase Technologies Corporation, a recipient in 1992 of support from the U.S. Department of Commerce's Advanced Technology Program (ATP) for their research on very fine powders composed of nearly spherical ceramic balls of uniform size, had just that experience. Building on research at the Department of Energy's Argonne National Laboratory, Nanophase knew that if they could make these powders, whose particles were only 100 billionth of a meter in diameter, they could use them to produce very strong industrial ceramics. The Caterpillar Corporation had expressed strong interest in using the powders in its diesel engines and was providing support for the early stage research.[11] As Nanophase scaled up their process from making 10 grams of material for $1,000 a gram to producing 100 tons per year at five cents per gram, the product specifications and costs suggested that a better first application would be with a cosmetics firm. Today Nanophase particles are used in sunscreens and other cosmetics as well as for polishing semiconductors and in structural ceramics, the original interest of Caterpillar. This experience is not unusual for a "technology push" innovation—a unique and interesting technology looking for the right first application.

Mark Myers remarked that: "specifications are really where [markets and technology] interact, because … you cannot make technologies fit to a market until you're really able to specify what the market requires. A major failure in programs is the interaction of technology maturation and change of specifications." Specifications in turn may change for a number of reasons, of which two dominate: because competition causes a discontinuous change in the marketplace,[12] and, as pointed out by Finnbarr Livesey during the workshops, because of "specification creep"—incremental revisions of project goals by the technical team in response to reinterpretations of market needs. For adaptive firms, rapid change and associated uncertainty create opportunities. The greater the pace of change, the more rapid the rate at which new information regarding market behavior is generated. The management of technical risk—the downside of uncertainty—involves a tradeoff between focus (precisely targeted specifications) and real-time flexibility (constant learning from, adaptation to, and anticipation of market movements).

Of course, appropriate strategies for managing risk also depend critically on the characteristics of the innovating organization. As Chesbrough and Rosenbloom observe in the paper that follows this chapter, firms tend to assess new technology opportunities in the context of their dominant business models. Large firms will view and manage technical risk differently than start-ups and mid-sized firms. Firms whose organization, capabilities, or culture are closely linked to a dominant technology are in a different position than new entrants proposing a either a disruptive technology (Christensen 1997) or a new value proposition for consumers based on existing (or only incrementally modified) technology. The manner in which institutional differences are reflected in the taking of technical risks is the topic of Chapter III.

Scherer observes that when you know what the technological possibilities are and understand what the consumer wants, you can go into the development process and write specifications with some degree of confidence. If that is not possible, you keep the spending low and explore the interaction between the technological possibilities and the needs expressed in the marketplace. Of course, by holding down spending, you may fall victim to a faster, more expensive competing project. You can deal with a competitor beating you in a small market, but you don't want to lose in a big market. In that case, you will try to find an alternative strategy such as a parallel path. Thus Scherer's model (Figure II-1) is not a profile through time of work to meet the four goals—technical reduction to practice, verification that product function will meet specifications, determination of probable unit costs of production, and defining all other market and business risks. Instead, it is a representation of the allocation of R&D resources to the four goals, seen in hindsight; the actual work skips back and forth among the four tasks. In fact the four phases overlap in time, and some work is concurrent right from the beginning of the project.

Risks of Not Succeeding, Being Too Slow, or Having No Impact

The paper by Hartmann and Myers underscores the point that the ability to clearly define a technical challenge depends on an understanding of the form the technology will take when it reaches the market. Thus, while technical and market uncertainties may be separable in a stable market, they will not be in the sort of rapidly evolving market that accompanies the introduction of a radical technology. One factor determining levels of risk is the length of time between the introduction of the technology and its market acceptance. As Marco Iansiti of Harvard Business School observes, the faster technological development proceeds, the more difficult is the task of separating technical from market risk.

In the workshop, Hartmann described the "Takanaka diagram," a plot of technologists' projections of the planned improvement of a performance or quality attribute against time. This diagram, which originated in Fuji Xerox, assists in framing the evolution of the development process. It addresses two kinds of risk—schedule and feasibility. This plan may also be contrasted with improvements expected in the state-of-the-art of the same performance or quality attributes that might be enabled by the technology advances of competitors across an industry. The research team on a given product has to be certain that it is aiming above that state-of-the-art trend; this is known as "competitive technology trend analysis."

In fast-moving areas of new technology, innovators chase a moving target. Speed is of the essence, and this requires the concurrent management of technical, product function, and market risks.

Notes

1. This distinction was made by Frank Knight. In his classic volume *Risk and Uncertainty*, Knight writes: "Uncertainty must be taken in a sense radically distinct from the familiar notion of Risk, from which it has never properly been separated... [A] *measurable* uncertainty, or 'risk' proper, as we shall use the term, is so far different from an *unmeasurable* one that it is not in effect an uncertainty at all. We shall accordingly restrict the term 'uncertainty' to cases of the non-quantitative type" (Knight 1921: 20).

2. Knight (1921: 46) writes: "While a single situation involving a known risk may be regarded as 'uncertain', this uncertainty is easily converted into effective certainty; for in a considerable number of cases the results become predictable in accordance with the laws of chance, and the error in such prediction approaches zero as the number of cases is increased."

3. One reader—a leading scientist in the field of neuro-psychopharmacology—observes that different stages of the process of drug development through "rational" design methods exhibit different magnitudes of risk as opposed to uncertainty. In the initial stages research occurs in the context of complex models constructed from fundamental molecular biological and biochemical principles. In the context of such models, researchers are able to arrive at informed conjectures regarding the relative "riskiness" of different research paths. In contrast, once development proceeds to the stage of clinical trials, no such model exists for reliably predicting the overall effects of introducing a given molecule into human subjects. This intrinsic uncertainty, as much as the daunting financial burden posed by the conduct of clinical trials, creates a significant barrier to entry particular to the pharmaceutical industry.

4. Larry Jarrett contributed the material for the two paragraphs that follow, describing the anchored scale and probabilistic methods for assessing technical risk.

5. The NewProd™ computer model developed at McMaster University and the PACE™ Complexity model developed by PRTM management consulting provide this kind of correlation with built-in databases.

6. See also Hartmann and Lakatos (1998).

7. The Scherer-Peck diagram originates from a study of weapons research. Note that, in weapons research, the technical feasibility phase will have a longer lead-in time (hence longer curve), and although such technology does not necessarily attain "market acceptance" in the traditional sense of the term, quantities ordered vary widely, depending upon the weapon's effectiveness in meeting emerging mission needs, and weapons developed for one mission often turn out to have other unanticipated uses. (Note that product specifications in military programs are normally quite rigid, while commercial specifications may evolve constantly, as more is learned about the technology and about the market.) At the

September 1999 meeting, Scherer identified in this context the example of the F105 fighter plane, originally intended for nuclear weapons delivery, which ultimately was used extensively in Vietnam because its design allowed for a relatively low-tech gun to be mounted on the fuselage.

8. This observation may suggest a dilemma for public policy. A government research contract, bearing part of a firm's cost but imposing an obligation for a best-faith effort to solve the technical problems, might serve both to reduce the technical uncertainties facing a project and also make halting the investment more difficult when trouble is encountered.

9. An option is a right, but not an obligation, to take a particular action in the future. Options are made valuable by the presence of uncertainty (Amram and Kulatilaka 1999: 5).

10. For an introduction to options theory as applied to strategic decision-making see Dixit and Pindyck (1994: chapter 2) and Amram and Kulatilaka (1999); for specific applications to research projects see Huchzermeier and Loch (1999) and Loch and Bode-Greuel (2000).

11. See http://www.atp.nist.gov/atp/success/nano.htm.

12. See Utterback (1994) and Christensen (1997).

The Dual-Edged Role of the Business Model in Leveraging Corporate Technology Investments

Henry Chesbrough and Richard S. Rosenbloom

Organized R&D in both public and private laboratories in the industrial world continually produces scientific discoveries and breakthrough inventions that open up manifold opportunities for commercial exploitation. Each of these events embodies the kernel of a potential innovation, whose realization requires investment both to shape the nascent technology to fit specific uses and to create the organizational capabilities necessary to bring it to routine commercial use. Those investments must be made—often many years in advance—in the face of significant uncertainties about the eventual commercial outcomes to be realized by the investing organization.

There is a common opinion that established businesses exhibit a systematic bias toward underinvestment in commercialization of novel emerging technologies, while start-up firms are believed to exhibit less of this bias (Foster 1986). However, the readiness of new ventures to bring novel technologies to market is accompanied by a disinclination or inability to invest in the initial discovery research and early development of those technologies. This puts more importance, from a national point of view, on the innovative behavior of established firms, especially the large ones capable of pioneering work in new technology.

Thus the sources of the bias of established firms against commercializing new technologies must be clearly articulated so that policy prescriptions can be formulated to offset them.[1] The social dynamics of large organizations sometimes play a role. In addition, the economics of "cannibalization" of established profit streams can deter worthy ventures. But other factors are also likely involved, especially uncertainty, and the business model, as we discuss below.

In the MTR Practitioners' Workshop in June 1999, most attention was paid to the uncertainties inherent in the situation. Clearly they are substantial and multi-dimensional. They affect estimates of key parameters, especially product performance, long-run costs, time-to-market, market acceptance, and competitive response. But uncertainty is only one element of the investment calculus. Investments are motivated by the expectation of future reward. Profit-seeking investors will commit resources in the face of substantial uncertainty if the potential payoff is correspondingly large in relation to the investment. In the end, the decision to invest is governed by the perception of that reward, its nature and magnitudes, adjusted for the perceived uncertainties and the expected time to realize it.

We argue that successful firms tend to interpret the potential value of nascent technologies in the context of the dominant business model already established in the firm. The reward to be expected from any innovative venture must be assessed within the framework of a specific business model, which will specify how revenues will be generated, from whom, and what costs will be incurred in so doing. In other words, technology does not create value in a vacuum. The established model may or may not be appropriate to the opportunities inherent in the new technology. If not, its use will lead to inaccurate analysis and underinvestment. That is one source of the bias exhibited by successful firms facing novel technologies, and it is the one to which we devote the rest of our discussion.

The Business Model Concept

This term "Business Model" is widely used, but seldom well defined. In our usage, the functions of a Business Model are to:

1. identify a market segment, that is, the users to whom the technology is useful and for what purpose;

2. articulate the value proposition, that is, the value created for users by the offering based on the technology;

3. define the structure of the value chain, that is, the network of activities within the firm required to create and distribute the products or services offered to customers;

4. estimate the cost structure and profit potential of producing the offering, given the value proposition and value chain structure chosen;

5. describe the position of the firm within the value network linking suppliers and customers, including identification of potential complementors and competitors;[2]

6. formulate the competitive strategy by which the innovating firm will gain and hold advantage over rivals.

Defining a business model to commercialize a new technology begins with articulating a value proposition inherent in the new technology. The model must also specify a group of customers or a market segment to whom the proposition will be appealing and from whom resources will flow. Value, of course, is an economic concept, not primarily measured in physical performance attributes, but rather what a buyer will pay for a product or service. A customer can value a technology according to its ability to reduce the cost of a solution to an existing problem, or its ability to create new possibilities. One challenging aspect of defining the business model for technology managers is that it requires linking the physical domain of inputs to an economic domain of outputs, sometimes in face of great uncertainty.

Value thus derives from the structure of the situation, rather than from some inherent characteristic of the technology itself. Increasingly, realizing value also involves third parties. The value network created around a given business shapes the role that suppliers and customers play in influencing the value captured from commercialization of an innovation. The parties in the value network can benefit from coordination if that increases the value of the network for all participants.

A market focus is needed to begin the process in order to know what technological attributes to target in the development, and how to resolve the many trade-offs that arise in the course of development, e.g. cost vs. performance, or weight vs. power. Technical uncertainty is a function of market focus and will vary with the dynamics of change in the marketplace.

Identification of a market is also required to define the "architecture of the revenues"—how a customer will pay, how much to charge, and how the value created will be apportioned among customers, firm, and suppliers. Options here cover a wide range including outright sale, renting, charging by the transaction, advertising and subscription models, licensing, or even giving away the product and selling after-sale support and services.[3]

Having a sense of price and cost yields target profit margins for the opportunity. Target margins provide the justification for the real and financial assets required to realize the value proposition. The margins and assets together establish the threshold for financial scalability of the technology into a viable business. In order for the business to grow, it must offer investors the credible prospect of an attractive return on the assets required to create and expand the model.

Case Illustrations

We provide brief case examples to illustrate our argument, and to show how the business model concept can inform our understanding when private firms can sustain high levels of investment (pharmaceuticals), when they underinvest in a new technology due to the use of an inappropriate business model (the Xerox copier), and when they overinvest in technologies due the reliance upon a previously successful business model (DuPont). We begin with the pharmaceutical industry.

The Pharmaceutical Industry: Sustained Private Investment despite Enormous Technical Change

One might think that the pharmaceutical industry would shows signs of strain from new "disruptive" technologies, because the underlying science for most drug discovery has recently been revolutionized, from organic and synthetic chemistry to genetic science. "Designer drugs" now flow from scientific laboratories in companies that a generation ago found their products through random screening. However, the industry provides many examples of large investments in new technology by its dominant firms. Many of the firms that led the industry twenty years ago (Merck, Pfizer,

Lilly, Abbott) continue to be at the forefront of the industry today. While there has been noticeable entry by young start-up firms, particularly in the biotechnology area, the overall structure of the industry is relatively unperturbed, especially by comparison with what has happened to leading organizations in the information technology sector.

Why has so much new technology created such little disruption? The plausible answer here is that the business model of the pharmaceutical industry has not changed much, despite the scientific revolution that has transformed the flow of new products. The value proposition for most ethical drugs is little different than it was decades ago, even though the science base and manufacturing processes for these drugs has greatly changed. Patents remain essential; the necessary FDA approval still defines the development path to commercialization; physicians remain the "customers" who specify the drugs to be consumed by their patients; and marketing channels to reach these physicians are still vital. These elements of the pharmaceutical business model have remained stable, enabling the industry to finance the commercialization of exotic technologies that draw from completely new areas of science.

Xerox 914: A New Business Model Required to Commercialize a "Disruptive Technology"

The introduction of the Xerox 914, the first plain-paper high-quality office copier, provides a classic example of our argument, both of investments deterred by the initial inappropriate application of an established business model, and of rewards amplified by the creation of a novel model in its place.

Xerography surely ranks as one of the most significant new technologies of the mid-20th century, yet its commercial success came only after it had been rejected by several leading firms, including Kodak and IBM.[4] Chester Carlson, a graduate in physics from Cal Tech who became a patent attorney during the Great Depression, made the core invention working in his kitchen in the late 1930s. After Carlson filed his first patent in 1937, numerous corporations expressed interest in the novel technology, but none was willing to invest in bringing it from concept to practical reality.

In 1944, he approached Battelle Memorial Institute, which soon entered into a partnership, investing in further development and acting as his agent. Commercialization was the work of Haloid Corporation, which approached Battelle in 1946 after learning of its work in xerography. Haloid, a small enterprise operating in Rochester, New York, in the shadow of mighty Eastman Kodak, served a niche market with high quality cameras and photographic papers for copying important documents. Its CEO, Joseph Wilson, driven to find a growth vehicle for his failing enterprise, "bet the company" in the 1950s on Carlson's invention. [5]

It was not obvious a priori what would be the best economic use of the powerful capabilities inherent in xerographic technology. Haloid first designed a machine to produce offset masters. This generated a modest revenue stream in the early 1950s. But Wilson saw the potential for massive revenues in office copying, for which the desk-size Haloid 914 copier was designed. At that time, copies were made for business use either by "wet" photographic methods, or by low-quality dry thermal processes. Both methods required special paper or supplies, creating an aftermarket revenue stream for vendors. Typical office copying machines sold for $300. The average machine in use produced 15–20 copies per day, and 90% were used for fewer than 100 copies per day. The existing business model called for charging customers the full price of the initial equipment, and charging them again for supplies as needed. The new 914 copier, which produced high-quality images on plain paper, had a manufacturing cost estimated at $2,000.

Haloid sought vainly to find a strong marketing partner for the expensive new machine, but was rebuffed by Kodak and others. IBM rejected the 914 after a careful and highly professional market analysis by the respected consulting firm Arthur D. Little and Co. (ADL). ADL could not conceive a successful business model, in part because they could not identify a salient value proposition. They reported that:

[because] the Model 914 ... has considerable versatility, it has been extremely difficult to identify particular applications for which it is unusually well suited in comparison with other available equipment.... Perhaps the very lack of a specific purpose or purposes is the model 914's greatest single weakness. (Arthur D. Little 1958)

Failing to recognize the radical character of xerographic technology, ADL analysts essentially assumed the 914 would be offered within the business model then extant in the office copy machine industry. Skeptical that customers would invest thousands of dollars to acquire a copier that would, after all, only be used to make a few hundred copies a month, they concluded: "Although it may be admirably suited for a few specialized copying applications, the Model 914 has no future in the office-copying-equipment market."

Having failed to find a partner, on September 26, 1959, Haloid brought the 914 to market by itself. It surmounted the obstacles of high cost by using an innovative business model. A customer needed to pay only $95 per month to lease the machine, and to pay four cents per copy beyond the first 2,000 copies each month. Haloid (soon to be renamed Xerox) would provide all required service and support, and the lease could be cancelled on just 15 days notice.

This was an attractive value proposition for customers. This business model imposed most of the risk on tiny Haloid Corporation: customers were only committed to the monthly lease payment, and did not pay anything more unless the quality and convenience of the 914 led them to make more than 2,000 copies per month. This let Haloid offer the 914 at a low entry price, to lure more customers. Only if the 914 were to lead to greatly increased volumes of copying would this business model pay off for Haloid.

Haloid's model essentially acknowledged that the ADL analysis was right, but was incomplete. Joe Wilson bet that ADL's conclusion could be reversed by a different business model. It proved to be a smart bet. Once installed, the appeal of the machine was intense; users averaged 2,000 copies per day (not per month), generating revenues far beyond even Joe Wilson's most optimistic expectations (Kennedy 1989). The business model established for the 914 copier powered compound growth at an astonishing 41% rate for a dozen years, turning $30 million Haloid Corporation into a global enterprise with $2.5 billion in revenues by 1972.[6] This was an early demonstration of a proposition now more widely recognized: that technologies that make little or no business sense in a traditional business model may yield great value when brought to market with a different model.

The story of Xerography in the 1950s is an archetype of what our colleague, Clayton Christensen, calls a "disruptive" technology. A technology is "disruptive" when it "bring[s] to market a very different value proposition than had been available previously" (Christensen 1997). Successful businesses, such as IBM and Kodak, have difficulty coping with such situations. Such companies, however, invest in many technologies, some radically novel, that are not disruptive. Christensen calls these "sustaining technologies" because they support growth in established businesses, reinforcing the complementary assets that serve those businesses. Successful businesses invest heavily in R&D for those technologies that they expect will fit within their established business models, as we saw with pharmaceuticals above.

DuPont Polymers: New Technologies in Old Business Models

Another example of the leverage to be gained by exploiting novel technologies through established business models can be found in the history of DuPont's many innovations in synthetic polymers. The DuPont story, however, also shows how the intoxication of growth through continued exploitation of a winning model can lead to an unhealthy overinvestment in commercializing new technology.[7]

DuPont diversification in the 1920s built highly successful businesses in rayon fibers and cellophane films. DuPont sold these products only to fabricators who turned them into finished products. As part of its strategy, DuPont established expensive technical support organizations to assist customers in utilizing new products. DuPont promoted cellophane—where patents gave it a proprietary position—to end users to "pull" the product through its fabricator channels.

This model was readily adapted to the commercialization of nylon, the first synthetic fiber, in 1939. At the time, the Rayon Department was the largest and most profitable in the company. To develop demand for nylon, DuPont helped hosiery companies develop replacements for silk hosiery, an application that sustained a premium price for the fiber. Similar technical support helped carpet producers and tire makers to introduce the new material in their products. The size, breadth, and scope of applications allowed DuPont to make significant investments in facilities for nylon, which, in turn, yielded lower costs, enabling development of further applications. This created a reinforcing cycle of increasing demand, which led to additional capital investment in production, which spurred further cost reduction, which enabled further applications.

The awesome commercial success of nylon inspired research activity in search of "new nylons," yielding the discovery of new polymers that were routinely commercialized within a similar business model. The first were Orlon and Dacron, brought to market in the early 1950s. Despite some concerns about cannibalization of nylon revenues, management wisely thought it better to manage the risk than to miss the opportunity (Hounshell and Smith 1988: 420). By the 1960s, enthusiasm for this approach had spawned a host of new materials brought to market in ventures following the established pattern. Some, such as Lycra, proved highly profitable, but others were later seen as poor investments. Corfam, a leather substitute, was a highly publicized failure; Kevlar, despite "miraculous" properties, was characterized by Fortune as "a miracle in search of a market," nearly a decade after its commercial launch (Smith 1980).

Implications

These cases suggest that the biases introduced by an established business model can cut two ways. First, as noted earlier, they can mask the potential for reward inherent in a valuable new technology to which the model is inappropriately applied. On the other hand, a model that has been notably successful in a series of new businesses can result in exaggerated expectations of the rewards from an innovation that has received insufficient scrutiny for that reason. The latter effect is similar to the force familiarly known as "technology push." In such cases, enthusiasm for a novel technology, especially when combined with hunger for revenue growth, can lead to investments in commercializing innovations without sufficient scrutiny of their true economic potential. DuPont's aggressive and insufficiently profitable "new products" push in the

1960s is a classic example of "technology push," fueled by hubris derived from highly successful research in the context of a powerful and profitable business model. A variant of this is the move to commercialization on the basis of enthusiasm for the technology itself, expecting that an appropriate business model will reveal itself in time.

In the June 1999 Harvard-MIT Workshop on Managing Technical Risk, Dr. Mark Myers described Liveboard, a failed Xerox venture of the mid-1990s that well illustrates this trap. Liveboard is essentially an electronic version of a whiteboard that is interactive and networked with other whiteboards and computers. An outgrowth of research on collaborative workgroups at Xerox PARC, it was soon recognized as a useful tool and quickly adopted for use within PARC and elsewhere in the company. A new venture organization was formed to bring it to market. As Dr. Myers described it: "we thought we would work out the business concept someplace after we got to market.... We knew there had to be [a market] out there... [but we] couldn't figure out how to make money." The venture was terminated in early 1997, after Xerox had invested tens of millions of dollars in attempting to build the business.

The Xerox Liveboard experience cautions companies to devote more effort and investment to identifying a business model when pursuing a promising technology. Unless a viable path to commercialization can be identified, money spent on such technology-push projects is unlikely to yield a positive return. In turn, the government should be wary of inadvertently subsidizing ill-advised technology-push investments.

We conclude by noting three implications of our analysis. One is that executives in successful firms weighing investment options involving novel technologies need to be careful to ensure that the intended business model is appropriate both to the technology and to the sponsoring firm. Applying an inappropriate model, simply because it is familiar (as IBM and ADL did with xerography), or proceeding without a clear business model (as Xerox did with Liveboard), will not produce happy results.

Second, disruptive technologies are sure to challenge the capabilities of established firms. An organization cannot simply shift its capabilities to suit a novel business model if and when a new technology demands it. Organizations will have to become more creative and more willing to experiment with non-traditional organizational approaches in order to respond to the challenge of disruptive technologies. In the meantime, visionary risk-takers like Xerox's Joe Wilson will continue to find opportunities to profit from disruptive technologies.

Third, government programs such as ATP need to look beyond technology-push-based applications for technology funding by the private sector. As the pharmaceutical industry shows, private industry is likely to finance even very expensive discovery-oriented research initiatives when those initiatives can be commercialized through a viable business model. As the DuPont example shows, a strong business model may even motivate private industry to finance these initiatives past the point where they are economically justified. We believe that currently, in the high-tech industries, the private venture-capital sector provides substantial enough support for the exploration of new approaches to commercializing promising technologies that depend upon novel business models.[8] This suggests a potential role for ATP: one that is focused on early-stage, discovery-oriented research and development, since venture firms do not usually invest at that stage. A potential ancillary role would be to support organizations that might experiment with commercializing technology through new business models in the many industries that are not now well served by private venture capital.

Notes

1. Note that we do not attribute this bias to firms of any particular size, only to those having substantial experience in a given marketplace. Size does seem related, however, to willingness (or ability) to invest in invention or discovery and in pre-commercial development of novel technologies. There, large firms are predominant.

2. The term "value network" is used in different ways by Clayton M. Christensen and Richard S. Rosenbloom (1995) and by Adam M. Brandenburger and Barry J. Nalebuff (1997). The former emphasizes the extended supply chain from supplier to customer; the latter focuses on rivals and allies in the "game" of competition. Both frameworks are relevant for our purposes.

3. The technology sector is witnessing a proliferation of business models as a result of the Internet. Models may be based on providing internet access to viewers, luring viewers with free content in order to sell advertising, selling

subscriptions to viewers, providing them with utilities, aggregating viewers and effectively "reselling" them to other content providers, selling products and services, or mediating market transactions between viewers. Some firms such as AOL blend multiple models together. AOL is currently an access provider, a portal, and a content provider, and is also becoming a market mediator. A newly emerging variant of this appears to be what is driving the "open source" software development model that has propelled Linux to prominence in network servers, where the code is given away, and supporting services are the source of revenues. This is a virtual analogue of the Xerox model used to market its 914 copier, which we discuss below. Our thanks to our colleague, Tom Eisenmann, for characterizing the different emerging Internet business models. See also Peter Cohan (1999).

4. Sources for this brief history include McColough (1984), Arthur D. Little, Inc. (1958), Gundlach (1988), Pell (1998), and Kennedy (1989).

5. Wilson spent $12.5 million on development in the 1950s, more than the company's profits for the decade.

6. In the 1950s, antitrust pressures forced Xerox to offer machines for sale and competitive pressures squeezed margins. The company moved to a different business model, creating an "annuity stream" from placements based on sale of paper and supplies and on service contracts. Hence revenues continued to reflect copies made.

7. The DuPont story is brilliantly recounted by David A. Hounshell and John Kenly Smith, Jr. (1988).

8. Particularly one very positive attribute of the decentralized exploration used in the VC sector to commercialize new technologies is that multiple parties will pursue many different commercialization paths and business models. This creates enormous diversity in ways to capture value from a technology, and allows the system to select from a wide range of business models in the case of disruptive technologies, it is far from obvious what the "right" business model will be to create value. In these cases, a system that fosters diversity is more likely to find a "better" model than a system where few models are explored.

III

Institutional Differences: Large, Medium-Sized, and New Firms

I believe quite simply that the small company of the future will be as much of a research organization as it is a manufacturing company, and that this new kind of company is the frontier for the next generation.
—Edwin Land, founder of Polaroid (1944)

Who takes the technical risks that result in radically new products, driving technological change and sustained economic growth? Nearly a century ago German economist Julius Wolf observed that established firms, heavily invested in capital linked to existing technologies, would have a strong tendency to resist radical innovations (Kuznets 1930: 32). Current thinking—consistent with the analysis of Schumpeter (1912) and a strong contingent of leading economists[1] and management theorists[2]—holds that that entrepreneurs and upstart firms drive industry evolution by advancing "disruptive" technologies. Many take surges in stock market indices (particularly the NASDAQ)[3] and the dramatic growth of venture capital over the last decade[4] as evidence of an ongoing boom in technology-based start-ups relentlessly challenging the status quo.

Yet Schumpeter (1942) also famously argued that established, large corporations—able to fund innovation out of monopoly profits—have an insurmountable innovative edge over small firms.[5] To be sure, in a number of industries—notably pharmaceuticals[6] and aerospace—small (even shrinking) numbers of established firms have been able to successfully leverage significant advantages in the size and scope of their activities into continued market success over long periods of time.

In this chapter we seek not to definitively resolve the controversy over whether large or small firms, new entrants or incumbents, are more effective in taking (and overcoming) technical risks. Rather, we seek to examine the ways in which institutional differences of various types (including, but not restricted to, size) affect assessments and management of technical risk.

Internal Development or Innovation by Acquisition

Innovations can be created from internal development, external acquisition, or collaboration. A firm relying on internal development assumes all the technical risks, but potentially benefits from the easier transfer and development of new technology to other parts of the firm, as well as from the possibility of stronger intellectual property protection. Furthermore, although internal development carries higher technical risks than innovation by acquisition, it can also be terminated at much lower cost, in cases where the venture in question ultimately proves unattractive.

An incumbent firm or new entrant can purchase a smaller firm that has already mastered a new technology and introduced it to the market. The acquirer's risk is less technical than managerial: Can the smaller firm be integrated into the larger without losing the creative capabilities, the intellectual energy and entrepreneurship, which initially justified the acquisition?

There are, of course, intermediate strategies: the creation of either a joint venture with another firm, or a partnership with a university and/or a government agency. While not as permanent a relationship as an acquisition, collaboration carries similar risks of incompatible objectives and culture. We address particular institutions for partnerships and collaboration in further detail later in this chapter.

Firm Size as a Determinant of Innovative Approach

Every firm struggles to find the right balance between internal development, external acquisition, and collaboration as strategies for creating products from ideas. However, that balance between the three approaches may be very different for firms of different size. The large firm may have the technical staff, the resources, and the patience to nurture internally generated ideas and bring them to market, but they must be grown from seed, so to speak. It may take too long for the technology to develop to the point where it will reach a large enough market to be strategically important to the firm. Thus the large firm will, typically, grow in scope by acquisition and in depth by incremental additions to its products and its markets.

A start-up company on the other hand—lacking the resources to acquire product ideas and technology from others—has no choice but to pursue a strategy of internal innovation, perhaps in collaboration with a potential customer. What it does have is a small team of people whose commitment is sharpened by their awareness that the company (though not its employees) typically has only one chance at success—as McGroddy notes, "you either make it or you don't." Communications within the team are close and informal, and the concentration on the founder's invention ensures a high degree of specialized knowledge. However, the communication between the product champion and the investors may suffer from many of the difficulties experienced in large firms. The entrepreneur has a passion to demonstrate the value of his or her idea; the investor is committed to realizing a high return on the funds for which he is accountable to his own investors (or stockholders). Correspondingly in large firms there is often quite a lot of tension between the creators and champions of a new technical concept and the senior engineers and business executives who are responsible for executing the product program with minimal risk to schedule and business success.

Mid-size, technologically specialized firms—companies that provide subsystems, components, or services to the large OEMs—may suffer less from this tension. (See Chapter IV.) Such a firm may be small enough to enjoy open communications and enough accountability and transparency to obviate the need for elaborate checks and balances in the management system. It may be large enough to have technical resources in depth, even including a corporate research function. If it is specialized in a technology and applies that skill to many markets, the firm may have a highly trained ability to understand the adaptation of technology to specific market needs. But the biggest advantage the medium-sized firm may enjoy is a minimal gap of information and trust between investment risk and technical risk. The same individual may be responsible for managing both. Lord Corporation, for example, specializes in technologies for controlling vibration and noise in mechanical systems; it sells subsystems and specialty polymers into many markets, from aviation, to auto assembly, to recreational vehicles. This business model is referred to as a technology-defined business model (Branscomb and Kodama 1993), as contrasted with models focused on markets, products, and systems. A senior executive of such a firm may be the leader of the technical team creating innovation opportunities and at the same time may have profit-and-loss responsibility with access to the company's capital.

David Lewis, vice president and general manager of the Chemical Products Division at Lord Corporation in Cary, North Carolina, plays such a role at his company. The dialog between innovator and investor is in this case quite intimate, since both roles are played by a single person. Often this will result in a greater capacity for understanding and evaluating technical and business risks, even when they are dynamically changing. Lewis offers some observations regarding the relationship between the size of a company and its strategy with respect to the management of technical risk. In a medium-size company, he notes, the relationship between the technical team and the marketing team is a close one: "the discussion is on a continual basis." He emphasizes that "managing and understanding the technical risks depends on how much you really know about the total enterprise, not just the technical aspects. The more truly knowledgeable you are about the market requirements and other downstream issues, the better you can assess and deal with the technical risk."

Choosing the Institutional Environment for Radical Innovation: Two Tales

The foregoing discussion suggests that the choice of whether to innovate new technologies through internal development, acquisition, or collaboration is made with the institutional environment (large corporation, mid-size supplier, or start-up) as a given. This, of course, is only partly correct. While large corporations in particular do make decisions within the constraints of fiduciary responsibility, history (including dominant products and business model), and corporate culture, technology managers may nonetheless choose to pursue a strategy of technology development based on the *internal* replication of the culture and incentives that define the start-up. Yet, as the experiences of Exxon and of IBM in the 1970s and early 1980s illustrate, executing such a strategy is no easy task.

Following the oil crisis of 1973 Exxon (like many other oil companies) began casting about for diversification opportunities. The information technology industry was beginning to take off, with the emergence of the personal computer, word processing, and spread sheets. Facsimile machine sales were growing very rapidly. At the same time digital PBXs were changing the way large organizations managed their voice communications. Exxon sought to exploit these opportunities by creating a new company called Exxon Enterprises. They purchased Lanier (which made word processors) and began making investments in small, technology specialized firms that were driving innovation in components for the information industry—solid-state lasers, optical scanners, new kinds of displays, semiconductor devices, and so on. Rather than pulling all these small businesses into a single big firm, Exxon Enterprises kept them as independent entities, hoping that each would be able to finance its own growth through innovation.

IBM saw this move as a threat from a potential competitor outside the information industry, but with very deep pockets.[7] Furthermore, IBM also recognized that this form of innovation through small, independent units, created by investment and acquisition or based on internal inventions, offered an attractive alternative to reliance on internal development pursued in a business environment designed for optimum efficiency in incremental growth. IBM tried the experiment, setting up three businesses based on internal inventions that would never be exploited through IBM's mainstream business planning. One was the blood cell separator, invented by an IBM Fellow whose child had died of leukemia. The other was an automated electrocardiogram machine, using artificial intelligence software to interpret the record of heartbeats. The third was an instrumentation company based on the idea that very cheap sensors could be used if only they were stable, despite the fact that they might be non-linear in response. Computer intelligence could compensate for the response curve and could correct for sensitivity to environmental influences.

None of these three businesses was successful, and all were terminated in due course. An analysis of the blood cell separator business showed that all the profits were derived from the sale of the plastic bags in which the blood was contained; IBM had bought the patent for these bags, but it was soon to expire. The EKG machine worked quite well, but IBM could not break into the close relationship of trust and familiarity that Hewlett Packard, the dominant firm, had established with the cardiologists who controlled the market. The instrumentation company failed to demonstrate sufficient cost advantage to be competitive. In none of these cases did the technology "fail to work." In all three the relationship between the technology and the market failed to produce a winning business model, and the entrepreneurs running them were unable to be sufficiently flexible to work around the constraints of their plans. By the time IBM recognized that it was unable to nurture an incubator within its own culture, the Exxon Enterprises business had also been divested for somewhat similar reasons.

Of course, a company like IBM (or Exxon) could be highly innovative when responding to its mainstream markets and competition. Exxon is the recognized world leader in petroleum exploration. IBM's invention of the random access memory cell, the magnetic disk data storage device, and the reduced instruction set (RISC) computer architecture are reminders of its ability to innovate within its core businesses. Such inventions, when brought to market, can leverage the entire volume of the firm's business, and thus bring returns measured in billions of dollars. At the same time, complacency—failure to be alert for technologies at the periphery with potential to destabilize dependable revenue streams—is still a very real threat to large firms in their core businesses.

In the essay that follows this chapter ("Raising Mice in the Elephants' Cage"), James McGroddy observes that large, established firms often fail to capture a significant share of the new opportunities in their industry, especially when they enjoy a strong, defensible position in some key sector. As a result they will lose market share to smaller, more agile enterprises. His explanation for this observation focuses on the different style demanded of those who would defend a known market with a set of loyal customers whose needs are well understood. This style he characterizes as playing chess: The game is complex, but the rules are understood and the ability to look many moves ahead will be rewarded. Science-based innovation, on the other hand, is more analogous to the game of poker: "This willingness to place small bets in highly uncertain conditions, using intuition more than analysis, trusting one's own judgment, is an essential element of developing a strong early position in new areas of opportunity."

McGroddy observes that a large firm with deep technical roots has some advantages over the start-up with limited resources. A promising new technology can be *incubated*, sheltered in the corporate research laboratory, perhaps for several years, without the compulsion to move quickly to market. When the decision to commercialize is made, the depth of understanding of the technology substantially reduces the uncertainties surrounding the technical challenges. But when the time is right for the project to be *excubated*—that is, made subject to external forces such as customer feedback, competitive capabilities, market changes—the large firm too often finds it "safer" to house the project within the structure of the existing business—the "elephants' cage" of McGroddy's title. Thus, technical risk takes the form of mismatch between the potential of the technology and the opportunities in the market, rather than a question of endogenous difficulties in science and engineering.

External Institutional Relationships

The institutional issues surrounding risk management are, of course, not confined to the firm itself, but include institutions outside the firm. Thus a smaller firm may compensate for the narrowness of its technical resources by forging links to one or more research universities. Or an emerging area of science with possible commercial application may be far enough from practicality that competing firms might well form a consortium to conduct early-stage research—lowering the costs and risks to each participant while at the same time requiring each to give up unique intellectual property rights and first-mover advantage. For the larger firm, innovation by acquisition can be seen as a particularly strong special case of reducing technical uncertainty by purchasing the innovation: the firm simply acquires a technology already developed and tested (although disappointment may follow the attempt to assimilate the acquisition).

The Role of the University

Start-up firms exploiting research-based innovations are sometimes initiated by the proverbial "attic inventor," but more often today are spin-offs from a university,[8] national laboratory, or sometimes corporate research.[9] This trend is rooted in the massive research investments made by governments, and nurtured by a government policy of strongly encouraging commercialization of inventions arising from such investments (Office of Technology Policy 2000a).

The phenomenon of new firm creation from university research has been particularly spectacular in the U.S. biotech industry, which was extensively nurtured by government funding. The Bayh-Dole Act, which allows agencies to grant title to inventions made with government funds in the universities that performed the work, helped to drive the biotech industry's growth.[10] Small companies were often able to keep afloat with government money for related biomedical research.

Such public research investments led to a new allocation of technical uncertainty between universities and other institutions. Mark Chalek of the Beth Israel Deaconess Medical Center notes that university technology transfer offices have become more professional, and while peer-review panels have not changed their standards much, clinical researchers have more influence now than they once did. Barry Eisenstein, Vice President, Office of Science and Technology, of Beth Israel Deaconess, observes that the pharmaceutical industry has changed from a "chemical-driven" approach focused on "working around previous patents" to a biological industry based on innovation. Industry in this case has moved toward the university rather than vice versa.[11] Nevertheless, the record of university success in gaining revenue from their research expenditures has been spotty at best.

Josh Lerner has studied the increasing willingness of universities to invest their own assets in the commercialization of their faculty's inventions (Lerner 1999). He observes that "universities have become increasingly interested in venture capital-backed spin-outs as a mechanism to commercialize early-stage technologies and to produce the greatest returns for the institution. This trend has been manifested in numerous ways, such as increases in the staff within academic technology transfer offices devoted to working with professors to establish new firms. The most dramatic manifestation, however, has been the proliferation of funds dedicated to investing in new firms spawned from these institutions." Increasingly, Lerner observes, institutions are seeing internal venture funds as an avenue to generate more wealth for the university. He quotes recent remarks by the director of Yale's Office of Cooperative Research:

It is even more instructive to look at Yale intellectual assets that could have matured into new ventures … like Human Genome Sciences or Incyte Pharmaceuticals. Each has a market capitalization in excess of 500 million dollars. Though Yale had the ideas, technology and personnel to form such a company a year or two in advance of HGS or Incyte, it did not happen because our development strategies were limited to licensing. (Gardiner 1997)

Table III-1, provided by Lerner, summarizes those university-based efforts that had actually been established by early 1999. It does not denote the many more organizations that have established such funds since, or are considering doing so.

Table III-1 shows venture capital funds sponsored by or targeted toward investing in particular academic institutions. The name of the fund, the affiliated institution, and the year in which the fund was established and affiliated with the academic institution are reported. In some cases, the efforts were abandoned before any investments were made; in others, the fund focus ultimately shifted to include other institutions or types of investments. Lerner notes that while venture capital has from its inception been designed to solve the difficult problems of the commercialization of academic

Table III-1 Academic-affiliated venture capital funds

Name	Location	Year Begun
Enterprise Development Fund	MIT	1972
Community Technology Fund	Boston University	1974
British Technology Group Venture Capital Fund	Various British universities	1981
Center for Biotechnology Research	Stanford University and University of California	1982
BCM Technologies	Baylor College of Medicine	1983
Tennessee Innovation Center	Oak Ridge National Laboratory	1984
Dallas Biomedical Corporation	University of Texas, Southwestern Medical Center	1985
A/W Company	Washington University, St. Louis	1987
Triad Investors	Johns Hopkins University	1988
Medical Science Partners	Harvard University	1989
ARCH Venture Partners	University of Chicago and Argonne National Laboratory	1989
Technology Ventures Corp.	Sandia National Laboratory	1993
Northwestern University Investment Partners [Evanston Business Investment Corp.]	Northwestern University	1993
Thermo Technology Ventures	Three U.S. national laboratories	1994
JAFCO	Two Japanese universities	1997
Southwest One	Virginia Polytechnic Institute and State University	1998

Source: Lerner (1999).

technologies, "efforts by universities to duplicate the venture capitalists' role by establishing captive funds seem unlikely to be successful."

University technology transfer offices typically focus on nascent firms in high-technology industries with tremendous promise. Unfortunately, these firms are also characterized by uncertainty and informational asymmetries, which make it difficult for the investors to evaluate business plans or to oversee the entrepreneurs once the investments are made. The consequences are often unfortunate. In some cases, the idea is commercialized, but the return to the academic institution is small; often these information problems discourage outside investors entirely and the discovery languishes.

Lerner observes that information gaps between the entrepreneurs and investors give rise to serious difficulties in debt and equity markets for university licensing offices. "If the information asymmetries could be eliminated, financing constraints would disappear. Financial economists argue that specialized financial intermediaries, such as venture capital organizations, can ameliorate these problems by intensively scrutinizing firms before providing capital and then monitoring them afterwards." Thus the institutional role that universities can play in ameliorating technical risk in new firms is dependent on the services of experienced venture capital organizations, helping to explain Scott Shane's observation. Lerner's conclusion is that

University spin-outs pose severe information problems for investors, which often can preclude the school from realizing much, if any, value from discoveries made in its laboratories. Venture capital organizations employ a variety of mechanisms to address these problems. At the same time, venture capital is limited in the geographic and industrial scope of the firms in which it invests. Numerous schools have been tempted to consider the establishment of funds that would duplicate the activities of independent venture funds, but case studies and empirical evidence raise serious questions about whether such efforts are likely to be sustainable. Rather than entering into these treacherous waters, university technology transfer officials and administrators may be better served by investing in developing strong relationships with the venture capital community, both with the significant local organizations and with the leading national funds.

Universities have, nonetheless, also provided fertile soil for new firms based on digital electronics and computer networks, not so much because of their technical prowess as because of the low barriers to entry for Internet-related businesses and the extraordinary levels of market capitalization many nascent businesses have been able to attract. Combined with the massive and consistent

investments by government in university-based biology and biomedical research, this phenomenon has begun to change the
culture of the research university, a change reflected in the career
ambitions of the students, who appear to be prepared to forego the
security of lifetime employment with a large, established firm in
return for the opportunity to test their entrepreneurial skills.
Similarly, faculty who were once content with consulting one day a
week are taking leave, or resigning their chairs, to exploit their
inventions. Thus the gap appears to be closing, between the
traditionally risk-averse university community and the traditionally
risk-prone business community.

Since government funding of university research, largely cen-
tered in NIH and NSF, is highly responsive to the demand of the
research faculties, any trend toward a faculty desire to carry their
research further toward proof of principle or even reduction to a
commercial technology is likely to be rewarded. Some agencies
appear quite willing to fund such work and even peer review panels
in some agencies will give it support. Nevertheless there are serious
public policy issues here. One is the fuzzy boundary between the
universal desire among members of Congress to see economic
value flow from public investments in research and the equally
strongly held nervousness about intruding into the workings of the
market as a mechanism for allocating investment resources. The
most nervous often carry the banner "corporate welfare" as a label
for their concern. We will return to a discussion of the government's
role in this triangular relationship in Chapter V.

Partnerships and Consortia

The research university, with its rich resource of knowledge and
talent, is only one special case of firms looking outside their own
organizations for ways to bridge the financial gap between science
and its commercialization. This search has led to a great variety of
institutional innovations involving third parties.

The mission agency partnership is one such innovation. Many
agencies of the Federal government have specific technical pro-
grammatic responsibilities, in health, environment, transportation, and other areas, which they pursue through research funding

in industry in order to accelerate the commercialization of new technology. In most cases these programs involve groups of firms in an industry, with government as convener and contributor to a pool of funding. One example is the Program for a New Generation of Vehicles (PNGV), managed by the Undersecretary, Technology, in the Department of Commerce, but funded by a variety of agencies in collaboration with US CAR, a consortium of automobile manufacturers. While the primary focus of PNGV is to encourage the major manufacturers to make rapid, near-term progress in expanding fuel economy and reducing pollution in passenger cars, an important part of the agenda is the exploration of technologies for new materials and new power plants (based, for example, on battery technology, fuel cells, hybrid combustion-electric, or hydrogen fuel engines). Smaller firms play an important role in these areas, with the larger firms tracking their progress and sponsoring their own work. The contribution of research in government laboratories, carried out in collaboration with the firms working through US CAR, helps to accelerate progress and reduce the risk of these new technologies. The tie to the major manufacturers enhances the information flow that might lower barriers to commercialization when the technologies look promising.

The university-industry consortium is a second institutional innovation designed to bridge the financial gap between science and its commercialization. During the 1980s public policy at the federal level focused on encouraging technology diffusion from federal research investments to commercial firms. Thus when high-temperature superconductivity was discovered, government agencies encouraged several groups of firms and universities to establish collaborative projects to explore its commercial potential. These investments might be considered pre-proof-of-concept investments, since the form in which the initial discoveries were made did not allow practical applications of high-temperature superconductivity to be realized. The hope was that by engaging firms at this very early stage the race to application might be won by U.S. firms. In fact most of these consortia were subsequently disbanded, but there is little doubt that many more avenues were explored at an earlier time than might have been the case under normal market circumstances.

In some cases government funding of an industrial consortium helped create a fund for investing in university research. Sematech, established to increase the productivity of the U.S. semiconductor industry by encouraging the manufacturers of production tools, allows the technical experts in the firms to identify areas in which the universities can make critical contributions. A predecessor organization of firms, called Semiconductor Research Coopera-tive, had engaged in the same activity without government funding and was superseded by Sematech. However, this university funding is intended to generate basic knowledge of value to the industry, not commercializable inventions. The Sematech program for pro-cess toolmakers did address the R&D needs of these small, special-ized firms, but primarily focused on creating more accessible markets for them through standardization of requirements and interfaces.

In view of the critical importance of the financial and research gaps as a risk element in radical innovations, it seems natural for government science agencies to provide some seed funding for research to explore the technology platform required to realize product ideas arising from government funded scientific research. Agencies might solicit the assistance of experienced venture capital organizations in identifying ideas in the university that merit this gap funding. Alternatively, government might agree to match research financing provided by the university itself, since many universities have created investment funds to promote the com-mercialization of their faculty inventions.

Radical Innovations and the Significance of Corporate Size and Structure

At the beginning of this chapter we asked: Who takes the technical risks that result in radically new products, driving technological change and sustained economic growth?

The foregoing discussion suggests a conjecture: Where technical and market uncertainties are high, small and relatively autono-mous business units—isolated from the elaborate set of checks and balances with which most very large firms manage their opera-tions—are the most the effective structures for nurturing radical innovations. This conjecture is supported by a recent empirical study by Scott Shane (2000). Shane finds that a new firm is more likely to be created to commercialize a new technology in a segmented market where patent protection is strong and core technologies are observable-in-use; a new firm is less likely to be the vehicle for new technology commercialization in older technical fields where a dominant design characterizes the market, knowledge tends to be "tacit" rather than observable, and complementary assets play a large role in business success. Thus science-based innovations that seek to create their own markets appear particularly strong candidates for new firm creation.

In a sense Shane's findings are counter-intuitive. The start-up is, almost by definition, severely resource-constrained, must put most of its energy into creating a business structure where none existed before, and has very little latitude for falling behind the schedule of investment and expected commercialization. Large firms, in contrast, have corporate research laboratories with scientific staffs, superior access to capital, and often a long record of having introduced innovations into their established markets. Furthermore they are often more effective than smaller firms at incremental innovations and at process innovation through which production costs are lowered. Why then do large firms not systematically dominate small firms in innovative performance? Analysts and scholars have offered conflicting explanations: planning horizons that are too long (for example, relying on amortization of production facilities to minimize costs) or too short (driven by Wall Street's demands for quarterly growth in profits); rates of development that are either too slow to keep pace with market developments, or too fast to allow emerging markets to mature. The very size of the large corporation may undermine its incentive to accept the particular risks involved in entering or creating a new market outside their core business, for the simple reason that the expected revenue and profit in the first five years or so are likely to seem insignificant in the context of the corporation's consolidated balance sheet.

Technically specialized small and medium-sized firms (SMEs), serving other industrial customers, may be more favorably constructed to deal with technically risky but attractive innovations.

While their access to capital is often limited, many of the more successful firms generate a lot of cash and reinvest much of it in internal innovation. Their goal is to destabilize markets by dominating their technical specialty and using it to displace more mature technologies used in industries they can serve. Most important, their management structures are built around technical leadership goals, and (as discussed above) the information and trust gaps between innovator and financial decision maker are minimal.

James Utterback looked at a broad set of radical innovations, and found that the majority were developed by technological challengers, but not market leaders (Utterback 1994). Yet, in their essay contributed to this volume, Chesbrough and Rosenbloom cite a number of counter-examples. The computer industry was started by IBM and Remington Rand, both established in accounting machines; the tire industry was changed dramatically by Michelin with the advent of the radial tire; integrated circuits were invented by Texas Instruments and Fairchild, both of whom were market leaders in semiconductors at the time. These various explanations and counter-explanations, examples and counter-examples, reflect the complexity of the corporate innovation process.

The bottom line is that large firms are capable of developing radical innovations. When large firms fail to face the technical uncertainties inherent in radical innovation, it is more likely to be due to damped expectations of returns than to possible penalties associated with technical risk.

Large firms, SMEs, and start-ups are impatient, but for different reasons. The large firm is impatient for the returns from the new venture to constitute a noticeable contribution to the consolidated profit and loss record of the company. The SME is responding to a timetable set by the original equipment manufacturer (OEM) they serve and by their competitors' responsiveness to these needs. The start-up is impatient to get the product to market under sufficiently promising circumstances that venture investors will continue to deepen their financial commitment to the firm's establishment. These differences deeply affect the way firms think about risk and reward from research-based ventures. Because time is so important to all three types of firm, the strategy for creating an innovation is often critical.

Table III-2 Contrasting the way large firms, technology-specialized small and medium-sized enterprises (SMEs), and start-up firms approach the technical risks of radical innovations

	Resources	Management style	Expectations
Large firms	Broad, in both finance and R&D	Structured for control of complex operations; evolutionary strategy	Material levels of revenue and profit in near term
Technically specialized SMEs	Limited but focused in a specific technology	Technical and business leadership closely integrated	Occupy leadership in technology specialty
Startup firms	Narrow in expertise; financially dependent on business investors	Structured for focus on specific goal; time is critical constraint	Anticipate IPO; seek to destabilize existing market

In Chapter IV we examine in greater detail the strategies used respectively by start-up firms, medium-sized suppliers, and large corporations to manage technical risk. The following essay sets the stage by describing the challenges to radical innovation particular to the large corporation.

Notes

1. See for example Kirzner (1973) and Baumol (1993).

2. See notably Foster (1986), Utterback (1994) and Christensen (1997).

3. Greenwood and Jovanovic (1999) find that broad movements of the NASDAQ over time can be explained in terms of successful challenges to incumbents by new information technology firms.

4. Kortum and Lerner (2000) estimate that venture-capital investment in innovation is roughly three times as productive as comparable corporate investment. A provocative paper by Gans, Hsu, and Stern (2000) finds in contrast that "while venture financing is certainly associated with certain instances of 'creative destruction' (the displacement in the market of incumbents by newcomers), the focus of venture capitalists on profit maximization and their ability to reduce costs of identifying potential partners increases the *relative* attractiveness of cooperation with more established firms on average."

5. A generation of economists following Schumpeter empirically tested various formulations of this hypothesis, but were unable to find strong, consistent evidence that large firms dominate innovation (Scherer 1965, 1984, 1992; Acs and Audretsch 1988).

6. In a study of research productivity in the pharmaceutical industry, Henderson and Cockburn (1996: 32) find "that larger research efforts are more productive, not only because they enjoy economies of scale, but also because they realize economies of scope by sustaining diverse portfolios of research projects that capture internal and external knowledge spillovers."

7. This case description reflects the experience of Lewis M. Branscomb, who was IBM Vice President and Chief Scientist at the time.

8. To cite one example of the stimulus of university research to high-tech innovation, Professor Robert Langer's 400 patents at MIT have reportedly created ten new companies. A survey of 179 research universities conducted in by the Association of University Technology Managers [www.autm.net] found that no fewer than 364 new companies were created in 1998 directly out of academic discoveries, as compared with 223 in 1995 and a cumulative total of 1,633 in the interval 1980–1995. Given the survey's fairly restrictive definition of terms and the significant number of non-respondents (70 universities, not counting of course those institutions to which the survey was not sent), these numbers should be interpreted as lower bounds on the number of new firms created out of academic discoveries.

9. Corporate spin-offs reflect the need to focus on core business and recognition that larger firms may not be well structured to take advantage of radical innovation opportunities their own scientists offer them. This has given rise to such venture firms as Ampersand of Massachusetts, whose CEO, Robert Charpie, specializes in helping create new firms from corporate spin-offs.

10. Because the passage of Bayh-Dole and the early growth of biotech firms were concurrent, it is difficult to assess how important Bayh-Dole was in that growth (Mowery, Nelson, Sampat, and Ziedonis 1999).

11. Cockburn, Henderson, and Stern (1999) analyze the determinants of pharmaceutical firms' relative success in adopting science-driven drug discovery.

Raising Mice in the Elephants' Cage

James C. McGroddy

The history of the last fifty or so years has provided numerous examples of industries in which opportunities opened up by major technological change have not been captured by the in-place major players, but rather are exploited by entirely new companies. This phenomenon, and the underlying causes, have been the subject of a number of studies and publications, prominent among which are Richard Foster's *Innovation: The Attacker's Advantage* (Foster 1986), and more recently, Clayton Christensen's *The Innovator's Dilemma* (Christensen, 1997). The increasing pace of technological evolution only exacerbates the potential for successful companies to miss major opportunity for growth. The focus of this paper, which is based on many years of personal participation in and observation of the information technology industry, is hinted at by the title. The central thesis is that the success of large enterprises in their dominant businesses is based on a culture and set of processes which are ill adapted to dealing with rapid and radical change in technology and opportunity. As a result, these enterprises more often than not fail to capture a proportionate share of opportunity in new products and services in their industry sectors—opportunity which in many cases grows to dominant proportions. Success requires that these new opportunities—the mice—be nurtured in a radically different environment from that appropriate to the large base businesses, the elephants. There is more than ample evidence that mice are unlikely to survive and prosper when raised in the elephants' cage.

Growth and Opportunity

The information technology industry, including its large component of communications, has for the past thirty years been a major driver of change and growth in the world economy, and is midstream in transforming at least the operational aspects of every institution in society. This growth of the information technology industry, in aggregate in the range of 15–20% per year, will continue for at least the next two decades, as the technology continues to surge forward in its capability, and the application and exploitation of these technology advances lag another five to ten years behind the raw technology advance. The improvement in the key underlying functional capabilities—processor power, memory chip capacity, disk storage density, communications data rates, and other closely related fundamental capabilities—will continue to advance at a rate of ten times each five years, a hundred times in ten years. The capability we have today is thus ten percent of what we will have in five years, one percent of what we will have ten years hence. This phenomenal growth is a near certainty, since precursors of these advances can be seen in research laboratories around the world. These large factors of improvement guarantee the creation of major new opportunities at every level of the information technology value chain, as well as "disruptive" change, in Christensen's terminology.

If history is a faithful guide, much of this new opportunity measured in revenue terms will be captured by today's major players, albeit with a very nonuniform distribution among the players. But a major portion of the revenue growth, perhaps half of the industry growth over a five-year period (during which the total will likely more than double), will be captured by newly emerging, previously unrecognized players, offering new products and services, building on new business models. More striking, these emergent players are likely to capture an even larger portion of the newly created market valuation. A look backward over any recent five-year period will confirm the plausibility of this view. The most recent five-year period has been dominated by the explosion of the internet and electronic commerce, both between businesses and other businesses, and between businesses and consumers, and the beginning of the major wave of pervasive personal use. Major new players and products have achieved dominant positions, including Cisco, Netscape, Amazon, America On Line, and the Palm organizer, to name but a few. In earlier eras one would have pointed to the growth of the workstation and the PC, with the consequent spawning and explosive growth of Microsoft, Intel, Apple, Sun, Compaq, Dell, and others. Even earlier one would point to the rise of the minicomputer and to Digital, Wang, Prime, and Data General as the leaders. Many of those key players are now either absorbed by others or otherwise greatly diminished. And it is important to note that in most cases the ultimate dominators of the newly emergent segments developed that dominance when the segment was tiny, early on in its development. Later entrants, usually larger industry players, often struggled without success for years in attempts to displace the early leader.

A key issue for today's successful companies is how to capture a larger portion of this new opportunity, opportunity which is barely visible at the beginning of a five-year period, often unnamed at that point, included if at all under "other" in market segmentations. The rate and magnitude of revenue growth in these new opportunity segments are such that without significant participation in them, large players, particularly those without a very defensible dominance of some key sector, will tend to fail by a large margin to grow at the pace of their industry. In an industry sense, they will lose market share. They will miss enormous opportunity to create value for their shareholders. Their failure to deal with the changed opportunity will, as history shows, lead to major business failures by more than a few firms.

Over a fairly long career in the information technology industry, I have watched many companies deal with these challenges, and I have had the opportunity to test the strengths and weaknesses of various approaches and to discuss them with a number of industry leaders. These experiences has led me to formulate a set of principles that are useful for thinking about this hard problem and developing guidelines and business processes to increase success.

Why This Is a Hard Problem: Chess Players at the Poker Table

Large companies—their cultures and their processes—are organized to succeed in doing what they do well: managing and growing large businesses, usually with a well-defined set of customers. In my parlance, they are very good at raising elephants. The processes used to do this are thoughtful and deliberate, rational, analytical, and quantitative. And because of the relative continuity of most large business sectors, the processes are designed to look ahead a number of years and develop plans that have a high degree of certainty of execution. This is a chess style of management. A good chess player does not make a move before understanding the likely sequence of the next ten or more moves. Analysis plays a large role and uncertainty is minimized. The experience with IBM's chess-playing computer, Deep Blue, demonstrates the degree to which this analysis can be codified and systematized.

What later proves to be major new opportunity is rarely wrapped in mystery or secrecy in its early stages; rather it is usually visible to all. However, the ultimate winners are not definitively labeled as such: they are mixed in a much larger pool of what will ultimately prove to be losers. As pointed out above, these winners usually develop a dominant position very early in the evolution of a new segment. What is very clear is that they do not do this with a chess-like set of processes; rather, they manage in a style which is much more akin to poker.

One cannot play poker without being comfortable with placing bets in situations with large uncertainty. The pace is fast, and one cannot take time out, or hire consultants, to get accurate estimates of the two cards yet to be dealt, nor can one learn much about the hands of competitors. The dealer assumes that the hesitant player has dropped out for that hand, and deals right by him. This willingness to place (small) bets in highly uncertain conditions, using intuition more than analysis and trusting one's own judgment, is an essential element of developing a strong early position in new areas of opportunity.

One of the major difficulties for the large successful company is the unwillingness of most chess players to play poker and their total discomfort with every aspect of the game. The chess processes, which have been proven to be effective in the main part of the business, prevent the person at the poker table from putting up any chips at the pace the hands are played. In my view, a large information technology company that wants to participate fully in the growth of the industry must, unless it dominates some major rapidly growing sector, recognize the need to implement a separate, poker-like, set of processes for capturing new opportunity either from an internal base, or partnering and investing in emerging external companies. The chess process will almost always come to "no," and even that will be at a slow pace.

There are many other reasons why emerging opportunity is not pursued in large successful companies, but in many cases they are results of dealing with potential opportunity by using chess processes. The new product, service, or technology is often seen as confusing to the understood customer set. It is often potentially damaging to an existing business model. In any case, the opportunity is clearly not large in the next few years, and the uncertainty is high. Besides, it is usually clear from the chess analysis that the investment required will clearly provide greater returns in the planning horizon if aimed instead at improving existing businesses incrementally.

In some cases the decision is made, despite the above inhibitors, to proceed with the development of a new technology, the creation of a new product, or the launching of a new business. As in the case of making the decision to pursue a new and uncertain opportunity, the typical large-company business processes and culture can be a major inhibitor of success in getting from concept and commitment to success in the marketplace. On the flip side, there are major advantages that are enjoyed by large companies in this process. The key is to develop, for each case, a trajectory of progress which builds on the advantages and avoids the pitfalls along the path of progress.

For an internally developed idea and proposal, even if the proposal is being pursued by others (as is almost always the case), one can usually identify two major phases of progress between concept and marketplace success. The first phase consists of invention, reduction to practice, the building of the first prototypes, and initial interaction with a few leading-edge customers. For a new technology, this can be a period of several years, whereas for a new application of existing technology the period is much shorter. It is in this phase that the mature company with deep technical roots has a major advantage over the pure start-up with limited resources.

I call this the incubation phase. In this phase the new concept is not subjected to the pressures of a going business, and it is nurtured and supported in its environment. The primary measures are of progress toward the prototype goals, aimed at first exposure of the concept to customers and markets. Typically the organizational focus of this phase is in a central research and development organization rather than in a line of business, and it is this phase that many of the large information technology companies have traditionally excelled.

Yet, having achieved success in this incubation phase, the new concept or product is still far from becoming a factor in the marketplace, and even farther from having the potential to be the base of major growth of an already-large base. Success is required in the second phase, bringing the innovation to market, and the challenges in this phase are quite different from those of the invention and reduction to practice phase. The level of resources, the types of skills, the actions that must be taken within and outside the company change dramatically, and often the level of risk, or at least of perceived risk, increases dramatically. It is often at this point, when the business players see both the potential for market disruption and the demand for significant resources, that the internal environment can change from being supportive and nurturing to being either overtly or covertly hostile. It is in this phase that many companies fail, and it is here that the incompatibility of the culture and processes of the ongoing businesses with what is needed for success in the new is the root cause of the failure.

The Internal vs. the External Path: The Case for Excubation

The critical decision to be made at this point, where the prototype and customers' reaction to have proven sufficiently compelling to drive a decision to make a major push toward the marketplace, is whether to proceed with an internal entity or to make a major move toward separation. I call this move to an entity with major independence from the parent company "excubation," a term designed to indicate the contrast with the incubation phase which it follows.

Incubation implies major, even excessive, nurturing and monitoring, as well as protection from many of the forces of the real world. From what I have seen, there comes a time when continued incubation dramatically increases the likelihood of failure. In addition to its overhead and its prevention of the creation of a competitively strong team, incubation often focuses the new technology on too-narrow targets of opportunity, those within the limited interest of the parent company. And it causes enormous waste of resources since Darwinian principles are not at work. An excubated entity, with major equity participation by its parent, can have the best of both worlds, but only if the control from the parent is restricted to that exercised by parent company Board members in their Board role. Experience shows that large companies do not easily come to the conclusion that excubation is the right path. Unless the new thrust is so clearly in the white space relative to the business unit's market and product ambitions that it has no interest (a rare case in my experience), the chess players will typically attempt to embed the new thrust in an existing organization, based on proposed synergies and economies.

I refer to this approach so commonly followed as attempting to raise the mice in the elephants' cage. The argument for doing so points out that the cage has plenty of room, and that it makes no sense to develop a new cage for the mice; besides, there is plenty of straw and food around, so it can be done without much additional expense; and certainly the elephant keepers will not be burdened by the additional responsibility. In reality, however, the behavior of the elephants will usually result in the demise of the mice. It is not that the elephants are behaving badly, but that in going about their normal business they are likely to either trample the mice (who rustle about in the night and really do annoy the elephants), or suffocate them with their randomly placed, but substantial, droppings.

While it is true that being embedded in a large company provides a number of sources of support not easily available to a small stand-alone company, there are several areas, key to success, where the embedded company will be far weaker than the stand-alone company with which it is likely to be competing. Key among these are the following. First, an embedded company, and its best people, are inevitably distracted by the monitoring and other processes that are part of that culture. This limits the ability to focus maniacally on a single goal. Second, the culture and value system of the larger company will typically inhibit the ability to build the strongest possible team. The creators of the idea are usually a good base for the technical team, but to get a first-rate marketer or business development person to join something which is tiny and not obviously central to the company's interests is likely to be impossible. The scale of the project and the size of the team affect the perceived value of a position in this culture, with the likely result that the start-up effort can only recruit from the second and third teams. Third, decision-making is inevitably slowed by the management hierarchy. Fourth, the pressure to get to market, provided in the stand-alone environment by the need to manage cash, is lessened. And finally, the ability to use market-value creation as a tool to both benefit the stakeholders and to attract a top team is eliminated. The net result is that often a team and environment are created which are markedly inferior to what can be obtained in a stand-alone environment.

All this is not to say that there is no value in having the right connections to the parent. Among other things, the parent can provide, on a very limited basis and on request, specific help in key areas such as the management of intellectual property or access to key expertise or tools. In addition, often there is the opportunity for the parent to be one of the leading-edge users of the excubated company's technology and products.

To get to a statistically significant data base to support the above assertions would be a major project. There is, however, in my view, more than enough evidence of the failure of major players to capture the benefit of opportunities where the key technologies and products have been incubated into an early leadership position to make the case. One example with an element of currency is the router business. In this case IBM developed three generations of products internally in its research division, and used these to build the early T1 and T3 internet backbones. Yet the anticipated conflict with the mainstream systems network architecture (SNA) products led IBM to pass on this opportunity. Recently, the last act of this drama has been played out with the licensing of IBM's technology in this area to Cisco, which grew to dominate the area, and which has a current market valuation which is substantially larger than that of IBM. An example of success for IBM is its creation in the late 1980s of a new company, with Toshiba as an equal partner, to enter the then-emerging market for flat panel displays. This company, Display Technologies Inc., is one of the major manufacturers and probably the technical leader in this multibillion dollar market, and IBM's linkage with DTI was one of the keys to the successful position which IBM has developed in the laptop market with its Thinkpad line of products.

With years of emerging opportunity ahead of us, and an increasing premium placed on velocity and being the early leader, it becomes increasingly important for highly successful companies such as IBM, Lucent, Motorola and the like to develop mechanisms for successfully creating new, major businesses from the results of their massive investments in research and advanced development. They must develop parallel methodologies to track new entities created outside their boundaries and build the substantive early linkages which create benefit for large company stockholders and customers. In my view there is a huge, underexploited opportunity to improve both these processes by recognizing the cultural and business process differences required to succeed in raising mice, some of which will, over time, become the next generation of elephants.

More Ways to Fail Than to Succeed: Strategies for Managing Risk

Venture capital investing is like a horse race. The technology is the horse. The management team is the jockey. The market and the competitive conditions are the race.
—David Morgenthaler

In this chapter we review a few of the myriad strategies used by both investors and executives in managing both the uncertainties and the potential rewards inherent in science-based innovation projects. For a particular firm and project, selection of the appropriate strategy will depend on such critical factors as the firm's size and scope (as discussed in the foregoing chapter); the nature of the target market; the quality of the information available regarding the target market; the source of finance; and the business strategy for bringing the innovation to market. Nonetheless, we do find strong support for the claim that portfolio strategies[1] are of limited value in a variety of contexts, not only in mitigating the downside risks inherent in science-based innovation projects, but also in enhancing the probability of exceptional rewards. In the space between invention and innovation, technologists, managers, and investors all have little choice but to manage technical risk at the project level.

The Portfolio Approach

As we have emphasized, innovation is driven by the anticipation of exceptional returns.[2] Where returns from invention may be reputational as well as monetary, returns from innovation are fundamentally linked to market acceptance. Consequently strategies for managing risk in early-stage, technology-based innovation must simultaneously address the risk of technical failure (failure to achieve required performance specifications within cost constraints) and that of market failure (failure of the product as designed to match market needs).

Why is this a hard problem? The reason is simple: There are many more ways to fail than there are to succeed.[3] This basic fact of economic life is borne out clearly in the essay contributed to this volume by F.M. Scherer and Dietmar Harhoff. The authors present data on the size distributions of financial returns to innovation at various stages of the innovative process (from patent application to public stock offerings) and in various industries. Their uniform finding is that the returns from innovation are "skew-distributed," meaning that "most innovations yield modest returns, but the size distribution has a long thin tail encompassing a relatively few innovations with particularly high returns." While "modest returns" do not necessarily signify failure as defined by any of the participants in these ventures, the skewness of the observed data on *ex post* returns does nonetheless immediately reflect the *ex ante* possibilities of innovation. Even when we take into account the exceptional talent and tremendous effort required for a seat at the innovation "poker game" and the cleverness (if not genius) of the players, the vast majority of hands actually played yield either a loss or a modest payoff.

Is it not then possible to manage risk by playing in multiple, unrelated games simultaneously? Or, perhaps, by filling the majority of the seats at a given (market/technology) table? Scherer and Harhoff report that such "portfolio" strategies for risk management have limited value. In computational experiments[4] based on data from Grabowski and Vernon (1994, 1996), the authors randomly brought a portfolio of 18 (out of a full sample of 98) new pharmaceutical chemical entities to market each year, giving each a 21-year lifespan. Their results for market return year by year for nine runs of the model show a wide divergence of returns from year to year (between a low of $1.6 billion and and a high of $2.6 billion in one run). These results, coupled with the raw data on the skewness of returns, together imply "difficulties in averting risk through portfolio strategies and in assessing individual organizations' innovative track records."[5]

The alternative to portfolio strategies is as obvious as it is inescapable: Build a system of innovation designed primarily to maximize the probability of success for each project. Risk management is an issue of *making* winners at least as much as it is one of *picking* winners. In the rest of this chapter we examine some of the strategies employed by venture capitalists, CEOs of start-up firms, and technology managers at medium-sized and large corporations in managing technical risk at the project level. We also examine the strategies employed at Trexel and AIR (the new firms described in Chapter I).

Venture Capitalists' Strategies

> The Horse Race: Strategies Used by Venture Capitalists
>
> Venture capital investing is like a horse race. The technology is the horse. The management team is the jockey. The market and the competitive conditions are the race. Wonderful horse, lousy jockey—the jockey falls off the horse. That's what happens to us about 60% of our failures… Lousy horse, wonderful jockey—the jockey gets all the ride there is out of the horse, but the technology hasn't got it. If you're using the second or third best technology in the industry, you're not going to win. Wonderful horse, wonderful jockey—but he's running at the county fair. They win easily, but the prize is $50. That is the small market problem. Very good horse, very good jockey, and he's running in the Kentucky Derby. Wonderful prize—millions in stud fees, all the rest of it—but he's running against the best horses in the world, and the best jockeys in the world, and if he isn't absolutely world class in both of them, no hope.
> —David Morgenthaler, Morgenthaler Ventures

Richard Burnes of Charles River Ventures (CRV) has spent thirty years working to reduce risks in its investments (Branscomb, Morse, and Roberts 2000). Over that time span, CRV's efforts have paid off. Statistically, risks have been reduced and results have improved. CRV has raised nine different partnerships totaling a little under $500 million, and has invested in 265 different, mostly early-stage, companies. (In the last ten years 80 percent of investments have been in raw start-ups.) Of the 265 investments, 55 have led to IPOs, and 45 companies remain in the portfolio. In the last year, CRV has invested $45 million in seventeen companies new to the portfolio. CRV at first was very eclectic, investing in everything from electric cars to biotechnology. In the 1980s CRV began to develop substantial expertise in the areas of software and communications. That shift has been very positive in terms of results. In Burnes' experience it confirms Josh Lerner's view of the information gap that exists between the inventor/entrepreneur and the investor. The successful venture investor will take the time and expense to understand the business proposal and its technical risks in some depth, or if that is not practical, to engage a staff or consultants with the relevant expertise.

David Morgenthaler's rules of thumb (see below) illustrate the venture capitalist's view of the financial, research, information, and trust gap, for this gap lies between the third and fourth item in Morgenthaler's list—the gap created by the distinction between when to "rarely invest" and when to invest "often." VCs do, of course, try to assess technical risk, and they do so by a variety of methods. Prominent among them are specializing in a few areas of technology in which they have expert staff, spending enough time with the innovator to understand the nature of the risks as he or she sees them, and insuring that the business strategy offers some alternative technical paths if the chosen path proves too difficult. But the most important tool is the advice of a network of trusted individuals who know the industry, know the technology, and know the innovator and his track record. The importance of such networks is well illustrated in the cases of AIR and Trexel, discussed in Chapter I and in the next section.

Another difficulty is the mismatch that often exists between the early needs of a new venture and the business model of venture funds, which tend to make substantial investments, even in young firms. A start-up firm seeking to transform a science-based idea into a new business must first get the technology in hand, while studying the market possibilities. This may not require more than seed money, financing in the range of $200,000 to $500,000. But Lerner (1999) points out that

David Morgenthaler poses the rhetorical question, "When should a venture capitalist invest?" His answer: A venture capitalist should

never invest to discover new scientific phenomena;

almost never invest to prove a scientific principle;

rarely invest to develop an enabling technology;

often invest to use a new technology to develop a product;

very often invest to revise and improve a product;

very often invest to produce a later-generation product;

very often invest to broaden a product line; and

very often invest to apply a product to another application.

The mean venture investment in a start-up or early-stage business between 1961 and 1992 (expressed in 1996 dollars) was $2.0 million (Gompers 1995). The substantial size of these investments may be partially a consequence of the nature of institutional investors. The typical venture organization raises a fund (structured as a limited partnership) every few years. Because investments in partnerships are often time-consuming to negotiate and monitor, institutions prefer making relatively large investments in venture funds (typically $10 million or more). Furthermore, governance and regulatory considerations lead institutions to limit the share of the fund that any one limited partner holds. These pressures lead venture organizations to raise substantial funds. Because each firm in his portfolio must be closely scrutinized, the typical venture capitalist is responsible for no more than a dozen investments. Venture organizations are consequently unwilling to invest in very young firms that only require small capital infusions.

As evidenced by the data displayed in Figure IV-1, the average deal size in venture capital has increased only since 1996.

This is a major source of the financial gap component of the "Valley of Death." When it is filled it is often from the entrepreneur's own funds or from angel investors, or as we shall see later, sometimes from a federal or state government agency. As discussed earlier, VC firms are, with rare exceptions, not a source of seed money, as evidenced by Figure IV-2.

For this reason some institutions have emerged, most often in regions where venture investing is quite active, that are intended to increase the efficiency of the angel investing system. In Boston and San Francisco there are informal networks of angel investors, such

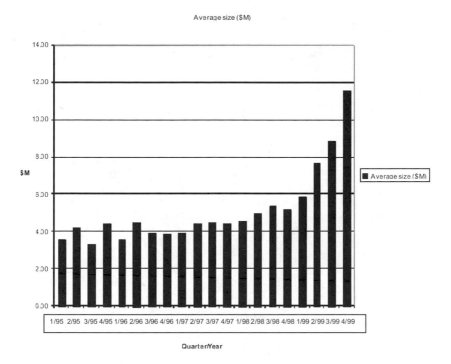

Figure IV-1 Average U.S. venture capital disbursements: 1995–1999.

as Silicon Valley's Band of Angels, that share information about emerging opportunities; in Dallas a large non-profit organization of VC firms called The Capital Network also serves as a match-maker between entrepreneurs seeking to start a company and angel investors.

Virtually all the venture firm executives who participated in this project agreed on one central issue: Their primary strategy for limiting risk is the selection of people in whom they have confidence, both in the technical and the business dimensions of the enterprise. Because their options are sometimes less than ideal, the firms take an active role in firm management, including using their financial position to require changes in leadership from time to time. "I can remember no case where we intervened to replace a CEO too soon," Morgenthaler said.

But risk cannot be managed independent of reward. The key to risk tolerance is the prospect of a sufficiently large prize that one is justified

Billions of U.S. Dollars

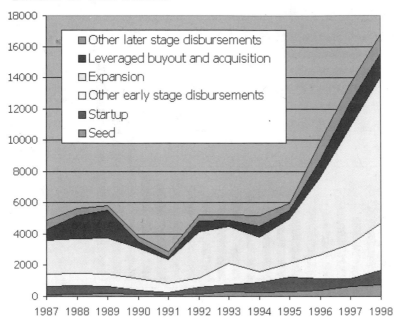

Figure IV-2 U.S. venture capital disbursements by stage of financing: 1987–1998. Source: U.S. National Science Board (2000: figure 7-26).

in spending what it takes to acquire the talent and the information to succeed with the technology. The key limitation to managing risks through fallback plans is the pressure of time. Investors are typically less tolerant of delay than they are of cost overruns.

Lessons from Two Case Studies[6]

Our purpose in exploring the two cases that were briefly described in Chapter I—the Advanced Inhalation Research (AIR) and Trexel cases—was to describe the evolution of start-up technology-based businesses and, in so doing, better to understand how entrepreneurs and their financial partners perceive and manage technical risk (Roberts and Gardner 1999; Roberts and Lieb 1999).

Trexel had been pursuing several different plastics technologies for twelve years when it decided to focus on MuCell, a microcellular plastic technology. The process is based on mixing a super-critical fluid with molten plastic under pressure. When the pressure is released, microscopic air bubbles are introduced and "frozen" in the plastic, at very uniform spacing and density. The technology offers the promise of reducing cost by reducing the amount of plastic material required by many applications. The case describes the new management team's efforts to commercialize the technology, and the difficulties encountered as they attempted to perfect the technology in various applications. The case also describes the various rounds of "angel" financing that supported the company, as well as various types of partnerships and licensing arrangements between the firm and plastics manufacturers.

AIR was founded to pursue a drug-delivery technology in which a large, light, porous particle carries molecules of a drug into the lungs. Chapter I sketches the initial research carried on at MIT and Penn State, and the early attempts to refine and commercialize the technology. In addition, it describes the venture-capital financing of the company, as well as AIR's early business development agreements with pharmaceutical companies, which generated both revenues and credibility for the firm.

AIR and Trexel are similar businesses in several ways. Each is attempting to exploit a platform technology: a drug-delivery technology in the case of AIR, and a plastic foaming technology in the case of Trexel. Both companies obtained a relatively small amount of venture financing to advance the technology, and each aimed to work with partners to develop, manufacture, and sell some products that flow from the technology. Thus, both companies have engaged in a series of licensing deals with different companies for different products. Both companies plan to use the proceeds from these licensing deals as a way of "bootstrapping" their way toward developing proprietary products themselves. Even though they are both utilizing a licensing partnership strategy in the early stages, neither wishes to be wed to this strategy. Both companies want to capture the increased value—and independence—that come from manufacturing and distributing their own products.

Obtaining More Cash at a Given Point in the Future

Both Trexel and AIR are focused on two kinds of future events: the manufacture of their own proprietary products, and some liquidity event that will allow investors to recoup their cash. Ultimately this could entail a public offering or the sale of the company. Each firm took several steps to maximize the potential inflow of cash associated with each of these possibilities; each limits the scope of the specific development deals and agreements it crafts with partners. AIR's strategy, for example, was to make "molecule-specific deals" (Roberts and Gardner 1999: 11). The company entered into an agreement in 1998 to conduct a feasibility study regarding systematic delivery of a particular protein. This partnership was followed later the same year by two separate agreements with two additional companies, each regarding specific protein molecules.

Trexel made deals that "offered exclusive use of [its] MuCell process for a specific product application ... over a three- to five-year period assuming the customer achieved production levels sufficient to generate a minimum royalty payment and garner a minimum share of the specific product market" (Roberts and Lieb 1999: 5–6). These terms were designed to insure that Trexel would not be "stuck" with a partner who does not utilize the technology in the market.

Each company, by limiting the number and scope of licenses, retained the rights to all other applications of the technology. AIR, for instance, was free to pursue inhalation drug delivery for all drugs other than the specific protein molecules it had agreed to develop jointly with its three partners. Trexel could continue to develop MuCell for any applications other than those it had agreed to pursue under joint venture agreements. Thus, each maximizes the amount of cash it may be able to generate from its own proprietary production. Moreover, by maintaining this large pool of "options" to pursue the applications it has not licensed, each company maximizes its potential value to an acquirer, or in a public offering of its own stock.

Obtaining the Same Cash Inflows, but Sooner

Simply getting the same amount of cash—but sooner—improves present value and returns. Of course, this is hard to do, but focusing on getting cash sooner is a common approach to managing risk. Both Trexel and AIR accelerated the inflow of cash (relative to the scenario of developing and distributing their own products) through licensing deals and partnerships.

Reducing Cash Outflows

In each case, the companies—and their backers—use several strategies to minimize cash outflows. One strategy for reducing the investment required—and for delaying it until at least some of the risks have been wrung out from the process—is to delay the formal start of the firm. In both the Trexel and AIR cases, substantial work took place in the university setting, with university research funding. Terry McGuire, the venture capitalist who helped found AIR, noted that he invested relatively little money ($250,000) up-front, but maintained the option of investing additional funds (Roberts and Gardner 1999: 2). He also pointed out that cash from the company's corporate partnerships allowed the business to minimize its ongoing funding requirements, and that this strategy continues to offer these benefits and minimize future dilution of shares (Roberts and Gardner 1999: 2). Trexel's CEO employs a similar model, "bootstrapping" via development agreements and using the money thus obtained to fund internal projects (Roberts and Gardner 1999: 4). Here too, this approach minimizes the equity financing required and thus minimizes dilution.

Thus, each company's strategy is based—from the very beginning—on one explicit approach to trading off risk and reward: During the earliest phase of the company's existence, when risk is highest and financing most expensive (in terms of dilution of the owner's interest), the companies minimize the amount of equity financing required by getting cash from another source: selling a claim on a specific application of the technology. This approach preserves the options for each company to pursue the unlicensed applications on its own. In addition, the partner-financed projects—to the extent that they are successful—demonstrate the viability of the technology platform, thus lowering perceived risk and the cost (dilution) of future financing. Similarly, by signing licensing deals, especially with well-known partners, the firms demonstrate the effectiveness of the technology to potential customers, and thus increase the perceived upside of the technology and the venture.

Obtaining the Same Cash Outflows, but Later

Sophisticated investors generally invest in a staged manner. They do not provide all of the funding sufficient to take a venture to cash-positive operations, but dole out capital in moderate-sized tranches. The objective of such a staged capital commitment process is two-fold:

• To the extent that there are multiple sources of risk along the path from proof of principle to reduction to practice, this allows these tasks to be tackled one by one. If a hurdle cannot be surmounted, further investment is truncated, saving the capital that would otherwise have been invested in the venture.

• If the hurdles are surmounted, the staging has the effect of moving the "average-weighted" time of investment back—closer to an ultimate liquidity event and thus, improving IRR.

• AIR's investor (McGuire) explained at the June 1999 workshop that "[O]f our total investment, $1.25 million went in after we had a corporate partner. This dramatically reduced the risk."

Reducing the Risk of the Cash Inflows

Both companies also do their best to reduce the risk—both real and perceived—of their business models. They do this by identifying the obstacles to the success of the technology and tackling them one by one. These obstacles are easy to see in AIR's case, because the FDA and the medical model are quite explicit about the various hurdles the company must surmount in creating a new drug-delivery method. AIR made very specific efforts to:

• prove the basic science by using the technology in an animal model (delivery of testosterone and insulin in rats);

• validate this approach by subjecting the research to the scrutiny of a peer-reviewed journal (publication in *Science*);

• prove that particles could be manufactured at commercial scale and at a reasonable cost (via spray-drying experiments at Penn State);

• prove that this commercial manufacturing process—spray-drying—would be sufficiently robust to work with the chemistry of specific drugs that might ultimately be used.

In Trexel's case, the risk seems to lie less with the science that underlies the technology, and more with the application of the company's technology to specific products and manufacturing processes. Thus, the evolution of Trexel's strategy can be seen as an attempt to reduce risk by reducing the expenditure of time and effort on projects that are unlikely to reach commercial scale. Trexel does this through a series of steps:

• canceling development deals that seem unlikely to be fruitful (Roberts and Lieb 1999: 5);

• focusing on more practical projects that meet Trexel's specifications and objectives (Roberts and Lieb 1999: 8);

• pursuing "fast-track" development deals that focus even more narrowly on Trexel's specifications and that also have tighter timeframes, further reducing the risk of an unfruitful effort. Trexel has refined its criteria to focus on "materials and applications that we understand and can transfer with little effort [where the] ... customer is capable of working independently ... [and where] the target product represents an interesting market opportunity" (Roberts and Lieb 1999: 10); and

• finally, narrowing the company's focus even further, in an effort to "control every step in the process" (Trexel CEO David Bernstein's remarks at the June 1999 workshop).

In each case, the perception of risk is a function of the context of the particular technology. In AIR, the medical model outlines the risks quite clearly. Company founder Robert Langer said, at the June 1999 workshop, "To me, what were the risks? Safety and efficiency, ultimately in humans." The FDA imposes well-defined hurdles, and uncertainty over whether these hurdles can be surmounted becomes a source of risk. Thus the key technical risks may lie outside product development itself but in the need to address barriers to market entry, such as FDA approval, or complementary assets required for business success, such as application software for a PC manufacturer.

In Trexel's situation, the uncertainties were more varied, as a function of the specifics of the material and product that was being manufactured, as well as the production process employed. Indeed, whereas AIR was able to perfect a single production technique (spray-drying), Trexel attempted to get its plastics technology to work in production processes as varied as extrusion and injection molding. This additional complexity and uncertainty undoubtedly contributed to its difficulties.

One of the keys to managing risk lies in mapping the expenditure of funds sequentially against the perceived risks. Thus, if the technical risks can be pulled apart into a series of experiments, and each experiment funded separately and sequentially, then the investor's risk is reduced because the investor has an opportunity to exit from a "failed" project before spending the sum that would be required for the entire project. AIR, for example, was able to separate the technology into a series of discrete elements:

- Can a large particle be made?
- Can it be inhaled?
- Does it achieve sustained release of the drug in the lung?
- Can it be made at commercial scale and cost?
- Will it break apart and lose its functionality during shipping?

Other technologies, for example Trexel's, may be harder to pull apart into a set of discrete technical challenges that could then be solved sequentially. Trexel's production of bench samples of the product at laboratory scale represents an attempt to prove out the basic underlying premises of the technology, but Trexel's technology seemed to encounter more problems scaling to commercial proportions (a challenge not yet faced by AIR's technology).

Other Lessons from the Cases

In addition to the issues that the cases highlight regarding the relationship between a new venture and its financial backers, they also shed light on the efforts of new ventures to attract the interest of another key constituency—partners. Trexel and AIR were both dependent upon development partners to commercialize their technology, and both faced challenges in doing so. Yet, in spite of their similarities, differences emerge in the two stories in terms of the success with which AIR seemed to be working with its partners, and the great difficulties Trexel was experiencing in this regard. There are several possible underlying causes of these differences.

Mindset of the customer industry. In many ways, AIR may have had an easier time dealing with its customers/partners in the drug industry because they were used to dealing with technical risk. The deals have milestones built in that assume there is some possibility that the technology will not work, and that give each party the option of pulling the plug. Moreover, AIR was most likely interacting with the Research and Development piece of its partners' organizations. In contrast, Trexel was dealing with a manufacturing organization, which is less used to dealing with technical risk, and where the pressure for current revenue is greater.

Modularity of the technology. AIR's technology (like, perhaps, most drug-delivery technologies) is more "modular," in the sense that the company's model is to find a drug with known efficiency, and then embed it in the company's specialized large delivery particle. This required a relatively minimal amount of coordination between the partners. While Trexel's technology might be similarly described as "give us your plastic and we will put the bubbles in," in practice far closer integration was required between Trexel and its partners. This imposes administrative and coordination issues on top of the technological ones.

Key external constituencies. One of the crucial steps in the process of managing uncertainty appears to be working early with key external constituencies. In many cases, this would include customers, but in the Trexel and AIR cases, the constituencies were development partners. AIR investor and executive Terry McGuire said that one of his main contributions to the company was to "get the company in early to see top people" at potential pharmaceutical partners. Robert Langer makes a similar point when he says that one of the ways to success in all medical-oriented businesses is to "get to the clinic early [and] get a real result." The value of this early involvement is suggested by comments of AIR founder David Edwards at the June 1999 workshop, when he noted that AIR's potential partners were actively involved in identifying many of the early risks: "There were many risks... would the particles break apart during transport?... [W]ould the chemistry of particle formation work with both fat- and water-based drugs? These, and many other questions, were posed by potential partners during meetings."

In the Trexel case, too, important learning took place when the company started working with its partners/customers. Trexel CEO Bernstein notes that "it is never a product until it is a product in the customer's product and process." Trexel's key angel investor, Alex D'Arbeloff, relates a more fundamental point:

You have to work with the technology to know what it is about... Applying technology to a market is trying to hit a moving target. Until you are in the market, you are not progressing ... the market may move in a direction that is unpredictable. So, the key is to get in quickly. When you are dealing with a technology, you have to hang in until you understand its advantages and applications, so troll ... spend as little as possible so you can hang in long enough to find your focus.

Focus. One of the main themes in the Trexel case—and one that was amplified during the discussion—relates to the issue of focus. Alex D'Arbeloff talks about the initial stage of a venture as the "trolling phase," in which you are hoping that some customer will bite. This is the phase where you are learning about the technology. The challenge, according to both D'Arbeloff and Bernstein, is focus. In D'Arbeloff's words, "companies that succeed, focus." But one challenge lies in knowing when to focus. Bernstein relates that he is glad Trexel did not choose to focus all its energies on two projects that the company's partners proposed—garden hose and coated wire—projects that were ultimately unsuccessful.

Risk Management in a Medium-Sized Firm

David Lewis, vice president and general manager of the Chemical Products Division of Lord Corporation and a Ph.D. chemist, describes Lord as follows:

Lord Corporation is a $400-million, privately-held, diversified company that designs, formulates, manufactures, and markets adhesives and coatings, and devices and systems to manage mechanical motion and control noise. Lord has three major operation divisions: Chemical Products Division, Mechanical Products Division, and Materials Division. The Corporation has facilities in seven states and ten countries and employs over 2000. World headquarters is in Cary, North Carolina. The corporation emphasizes four core technologies: material science; electro-mechanical dynamic systems; chemical synthesis and polymerization; and surface science. It applies these technologies to develop, manufacture and market unique, high-quality products that bring high value to its customers in selected niche markets. (Lewis 2000)

He notes that firms are always looking for protectable, radical innovations that offer the possibility of destabilizing existing markets. However, the company can, to some extent, manage risk by holding a diversified portfolio of R&D projects: a "mix of flyers, mid-risk projects, and low-risk." This is not an assertion that SMEs can expect to follow a portfolio strategy, but rather that the smaller the firm the more attention must be paid to how business uncertainties are aggregated. On a rare occasion a firm may chose to "bet the company" by taking a high level of technical uncertainty, associated with a level of investment that threatens the firm's liquidity. This is only likely to happen when the conditions Lewis described below in Case A are present.

Lewis emphasizes that understanding the market can be as important for managing technical risk as understanding the technology, the point we emphasized in Chapter II. Where market knowledge is deep, technical risk is easier to manage, because, as discussed earlier, one has confidence in one's understanding of the requirements of the market. If you know what the product specifications have to be, you will know when the technology will not support them, and you can stop, at least temporarily. Halting a project that is doomed to disappointment is a key element of risk management. The risk model shown in Figure I-2 shows that if a project doomed to failure is halted during the first stage of technical research the opportunity cost is relatively modest. However, failing to pursue a project simply because product requirements are as yet undefined and are a function of both technical and market uncertainties is to fail in technical risk management. This is the failure to which large firms are often prey, as discussed by McGroddy.

David Lewis (2000) has offered the following three cases, drawn from his company's experience, in which technical uncertainties were evaluated and projects initiated.

Case A: Technology Push with Understood Market Requirements and Controlled Commercialization

Case A is an example of "technology push" in the basic concept stage. A major project that evolved from an in-house technical invention, it involved the invention and commercialization of a major new product line of environmentally acceptable adhesives for bonding rubber to metal. The concept had been developed by one of our scientists and was a classic technical-push situation. The technology was in an area of high familiarity to the company: Lord has been the global leader in the technology for bonding rubber to metal for over forty years, and probably has a better knowledge of the market requirements and in-house testing than many of its customers. Thus, the company had a tremendous capability to understand technical risk of later phases from the outset. We knew that it would be the most difficult technical project the company had had in many, many years, and that it would have the highest expense of any project to date (the total project cost, including building a stand-alone plant, represented the largest investment the Chemical Products Division had made in its history).

Fortunately in this case the company also had the best handle on technical risk at each stage that it had ever had. Concept risk was minimal, as this was a case of technology push. We could go through steps such as in-house testing that allowed us to minimize the risk exposure for the Corporation at every level while verifying our ability to meet market requirements. Commercialization of both the production process and the product introductions were done via avenues in which the company had considerably experience.

This was a good example of what from the outside appeared to be a very high technical risk project, but one that could in fact be managed and controlled very well, due to the company's very strong technical knowledge base in all three phases. Unlike most technical push projects, which face major market requirement questions, our first-hand knowledge of market requirements reduced those issues significantly.

Case B: Market Pull with Available Invention, Poorly Defined Market Requirements, and Capable Commercialization

Case B illustrates how the extent of a company's understanding of market requirements can have a major impact on technical risk. This is an example of a direct articulated need by a customer, in the general area of adhesives for auto assembly where Lord is currently a supplier. Specifically it was for an application that was both new to us and in some respects a major extension for our customer. What appeared to be a good technical invention was in place and we moved well down the path of specific product commercialization. Market requirements, however, soon became a major difficulty: the requirements were initially detailed by the customer but changed with time and understanding. Further final application testing was available only at the customer's location, and special tests were added during the protocol. We were thus vulnerable to surprises that came out of the customer's work, as testing went on and as the customer's understanding of requirements, and ours, evolved. Well into the project, a new test was put in place that our product could not pass. In previous instances, we had been able to modify our base technical approach to achieve success, but the new requirement was such that our base invention technology was now unsuitable for the application. It was a surprise to us, a curve ball that completely changed our original assessment of technical risk, because the market requirements were now different. It essentially put us back to square one, searching for a new technical innovation that could meet the new requirements. This is an example of a case where technical risk was considered and understood at project inception, but where technical risk changed drastically with changing understanding of market requirements.

Case C: Market Pull with High Technical Risk at the Invention Phase

Case C relates to an effort to develop a breakthrough approach to commercial floor coatings. Unlike Case A, which was technology push, this is an example of market pull. This is a classic situation for a company that is an established player in a market and feels that they can have a very, very successful product if they can make a major breakthrough in one or two key technical areas. In this case, the "pot of gold" was large enough that we were willing to take a technical flyer on some ideas and essentially fund an applied research program without a truly identified technical solution at the onset of the project. Because of the large commercial potential, a significant effort was felt justifiable and was in fact mounted. We did not, in the end, develop the basic invention breakthrough we had hoped for, but that was part of the calculation: we were willing to spend a certain amount of money trying some unusual approaches to solve the problem. This is an example where technical risk was large, and in some respects unquantifiable, because of the unknowns involved in seeking out a new technical invention. That was balanced by what was perceived to be a low risk in both market requirements and commercialization if we were to get to those points.

It is important to note that, despite its initial lack of success, we have buried this experiment in a shallow grave. This is a familiar type of situation in the laboratory, and if one of our scientists comes up with a better idea further down the road, it's something we will resurrect.

Risk Characterization in a Larger Firm

Some firms have developed formal systems for risk evaluation as a means for ensuring that risk and reward are in appropriate balance. The system developed at Xerox by George Hartmann and Mark Myers was designed to deal with innovation in large company with a very active research and innovation program. Xerox has on the order of 300 investments at a time, at different stages through the pipeline. These investments have to be spread over a portfolio of new or existing markets and technology in order to balance the risks. Hartmann and Myers, in their essay, categorize the different levels of risk/return projects in these classes:

• *Evolutionary business offerings* (existing markets, existing technology): Lowest risk, but also limited economic potential;

• *Leverage base extensions* (new markets, existing technologies): For a global company, opportunities of this type tend to be geographical;

• *Discontinuities in technology* (existing markets, new technology): This is what we are most familiar with: technological substitution;

• *Radical innovations* (new markets, new technologies): Low probability outcome, but holds greatest opportunity.

These differences do not fully describe the differences in risk to be found within the firm's portfolio of projects. Other significant parameters of the risk equation, as Hartmann and Myers describe them, include:

• *Competence:* "Sometimes you have access to the technology, but ... you're not competent as an organization [to be a player in the area]."

• *Specifications:* "Specifications are ... where these two sides interact.... [Y]ou cannot make technologies fit to a market until you're really able to specify what the market requires. A major failure in programs is the interaction of technology maturation and change of specifications. Why do specifications change? Because competition causes a disruption in the marketplace."

- *Complementary assets:* "Are there other people in the industry helping to develop the complementary parts of the technology that you need, particularly at a systems level?"

- *Value chain:* "Do you have access to the complete value chain to serve the market?"[7]

- *Market preparedness:* "Is there a customer base prepared to use the technology?"

- *Business concept:* "How do you make money?" Corporations move away from their business concepts very reluctantly, as discussed in the essay by Henry Chesbrough and Richard Rosenbloom.

Do individual technology managers tend to be more risk-averse than would be ideal from the perspective of the organization as a whole? If so, does this lead to an overall bias against undertaking enough high-risk projects? Myers replies that products following the evolutionary path in the innovation typology presented above tend to become commodities, but "a technology company does not want to work in commodity space." Consequently, there are strong incentives within a large corporation to invest in projects that represent at least discontinuities, if not radical innovations. This is what David Lewis refers to as products that "destabilize the market."

Xerox makes a series of investments in speculative research projects where it is not always clear what will come out of the work, funded by corporate headquarters from protected funds. Technology development begins with technology concept initiation (a negotiated collaboration between corporate research and the business divisions). Product concept initiation then begins commitment to product generation. At the end of phase 2, the concept phase, Hartmann and Myers observe, "the technology has been shown to be capable of meeting the performance requirements, to be manufacturable, and to be sufficiently robust that it is ready to begin product design, which usually requires a significant ramp-up of product development resources." This represents successfully transiting the R&D gap.

Risk Management in a Very Large Firm

McGroddy identifies three phases in technology project management with a very large firm:

1. *Discovery and invention phase:* Often pursued in a corporate research laboratory. This phase holds the most interest for the scientists and creates expectations for commercial reward, but without testing the likelihood of reaping that reward.

2. *Incubation:* Investing in the technology, protected from normal marketplace values. The firm does not insist on making money at this stage, but early exposure to the intended marketplace helps direct the research. This is the research required to bridge the gap.

3. *Excubation:* Ramp up production within the company or develop the technology outside the company through "excubation" (which McGroddy contrasts with "sheltered incubation" of a new technology). At this point the possibility of "fratricide" (competition with one of the company's established products) arises. As an example of "excubation," McGroddy cites the very successful experience of IBM in its joint venture with Toshiba to manufacture and market flat panel displays, which would, if developed internally, be seen as competing with technologically inferior IBM gas-panel displays.[8]

4. Another excubation strategy is to spin out the invention to a small firm or start-up outside the company.

The company has to manage technical risk differently in each of the above three phases. In the first phase the primary failure is, "the stuff won't work." In the second phase you start to engage the question of whether the technology will or will not be producible at an acceptable cost and meet a market need. In the third phase, the manager has to either match the product with the existing activities of the company, or move to develop the product outside the company. There are several reasons to develop the product outside the company:

• The product may be very important to the company in the long run and external development may be the quickest way to pursue it in an environment protected from internal competition, as in the case of the flat panel display venture with Toshiba.

• "You owe it to the people." If you show your willingness to pursue innovations, even when they do not fit core business priorities, you can hire people who are entrepreneurs, who want to make something happen in the marketplace. "You can build that kind of an image for your company."

• It is important to expose technology early to surrogates for what the market will be. Of course, one has to be careful in the selection of the surrogates; the government is normally a poor surrogate because its market requirements are more arbitrary, less cost-sensitive, and may not represent leading-edge user needs.

• Basic research should be exposed to potential applications very early on. As a rule, researchers are enthusiastic about this.

• Going outside may help in understanding the internal conflicts within the company, such as displacement threat, competition for resources, or distraction to the customers in the marketplace.

• The company may actually make a lot of money from businesses started outside its walls.[9]

Finally, firms must beware of intellectual arrogance. When technology "fails," the team concludes that the task must be impossible because "we, the smartest people in the industry, couldn't make it work." As David Morgenthaler said, "We look at availability of alternative technical solutions. If this one fails, what's our alternative? We compare [our technology] with the competitive technology. Why are we so smart? Why are we better off than IBM and Xerox and all the other people who have been out there putting a lot of effort on it? I find that when I'm smarter than anybody, I'd better go back and re-examine what we're doing."

Other Corporate Strategies for Risk Management

A variety of other techniques for minimizing risk without reducing the potential reward are used by high-tech firms in the United States and Japan. Let us consider several of them. The first deals with the strategy for introducing a new science-based technology into a consumer market. This is a very different situation from that discussed in the previous section, in which the innovations were all office or industrial products. Consumer products are characterized by very large volumes and very tight cost pressure on the producer.

"Trickle-up Technology": Reducing Technical Risks in Consumer Markets

When introducing a new research-based technology to a consumer product market, the market requirements for large volume and low cost define the character of technical risk. Not only must the product function be right, but the process technology used to manufacture it must be capable of high production yields and very low production cost. The usual American strategy is to introduce the technology first in the most sophisticated, price-insensitive end of a product line, perhaps in a commercial use, not a consumer use. This allows one to take maximum advantage of the qualitative advantages the technology may have over conventional technology. It finds application where customers who appreciate the new function will tolerate high early production costs, and involves relative low production volumes that do not require high manufacturing yield.

Experience in production gives rise to higher yield and thus lower costs through what is called the production "learning curve" (see, e.g., Auerswald et al. 2000). In due course, a less expensive version of the technology, perhaps of somewhat lower performance, can be introduced in a mid-range, higher-volume application. Eventually the technology will find its way into consumer products. In this way the technology "trickles down" from high-performance, high-cost uses to low-cost mass production for the consumer market. In the process, the first-mover advantage may be lost, since this migration of the technology from low-volume, high-priced markets to a consumer market can take many years.

Many of the most successful Japanese consumer electronics firms pursued a strategy in the 1980s we call, by contrast, "trickle-up" technology introduction.[10] The best example is, perhaps, the charge-coupled device (CCD) display, now used in every laptop computer at very high levels of performance (high resolution, color, and rapid writing speed). The Japanese introduced CCD technology first in a digital wristwatch, where only four characters were required, gray and white, changing only once a second, on a tiny screen. Their approach recognized that the largest source of technical risk for CCD technology is likely to lie in the producability of the product, especially if the depth of understanding of CCD technology is still immature. The wristwatch performance requirements were much more modest than the CCD science, at least theoretically, allowed. This lowered the risk. But the wristwatch application required that hundreds of thousands of displays be produced. The technology then followed a performance-enhancing learning curve, rather than a cost-reducing one. The next generation of the product would have higher performance, but costs would rise slowly as performance rose. Thus the technology would "trickle up" from a consumer commodity to a higher performance business application. When two competitors introduced the same technology (for example IBM with "trickle-down" and Sharp Corp. with "trickle-up"), and they met one another in an intermediate-level market with the same performance requirements, it was almost certain that the Sharp production would be at considerably lower cost.

Thus the nature of the market can determine the relative importance of process versus performance specifications, and this will substantially influence the priorities for addressing issues of technical uncertainty and risk.

Sharing Risks with the Customer: Supply Chain Integration

In David Lewis's discussion of his third case, earlier in this chapter, he noted that the primary source of technical risk was the fact that his customer, a large OEM (an auto maker), did not have stable requirements. As the requirements changed, they finally grew outside the performance window of the new technology the Lord Corporation was proposing to offer as the solution. Dr. Lewis was ultimately forced to "bury the project in a shallow grave," awaiting a new idea from his research team that would meet the customer's need.

While this episode proved disappointing to Lord, it is noteworthy that as Lewis tells the story, Lord engineers and chemists are in very close contact with the customer's technical people; they were addressing the match of market need and technology performance together. When this kind of supplier-OEM collaboration is supported by modern information technology, which allows co-development at a distance, we have what is called "supply chain integration." This is a key strategy for reducing technical risks of high-tech suppliers to demanding customers. Note that the inventor/entrepreneur in this case is the supplier firm. But the investor, the customer firm, is represented by his technical team, under the supervision of the OEM's product manager. Thus supply chain integration gives the possibility of narrowing the information gap that otherwise would plague the inventor and finance officers of a large enterprise. However, the key for this to work, as Lewis points out in his discussion of Case B, is that both partners, the supplier and the OEM, must share a correct and detailed understanding of the specific technical market requirements that will govern the final phases of commercialization. The ability of both parties to estimate and manage technical risk in the later phases (market requirements and robust commercialization) is highly dependent upon this capacity.

Linkages to Experts: Consultants, Universities, Other Laboratories

At the end of Chapter III, we identified institutional relationships outside the firm as a way to compensate for the disadvantages the firms of different size and age might experience. Technical risk of large firms (OEMs) can be reduced by sharing the research challenges with suppliers (as we have just seen in supply chain integration, where we looked through the eyes of the supplier). But firms can also share with their competitors, through a variety of mechanisms, or with not-for-profit third parties, such as research laboratories. At the technical level, they will, of course, look to the most advanced research institutes and university laboratories for consultants to help them when they encounter technical difficulties. The use of consultants is, of course, only an alternative to hiring those skills into the project team. But it may be preferable because the level of skill may not be available for recruiting to the firm, or because the firm may not wish to commit itself to that level of skill in the event the project fails.[11]

We examined in Chapter III the linkage with universities, for example through continuing research sponsored by the firm as means of risk reduction. We took the view of the universities, which, in the United States at least, are eager to see the inventions of their faculty recognized, with concomitant revenue to the hard-pressed universities. Here we look briefly at these linkages from the perspective of the firm.

We have discussed the gap in information, and perhaps in trust, that may occur between an inventor and the VC or between inventors in a firm and the executives who can commit financial resources to the new project. When an existing firm looks at the opportunity to finance research at a university, with the hope of generating inventions that the firm might commercialize, this gap may become a chasm, perhaps better described as a gap in corporate cultures. The firm and the university have such different purposes, and their people such different expectations, that it may be hard to achieve the conditions for common goals and common understandings about how the two institutions are to collaborate while each pursues its own program. This issue has been discussed extensively elsewhere (Branscomb, Kodama, and Florida 1999).

It is worth observing that most of the activity in corporate support for academic research, where there are expectations on both sides for commercial outcomes, is in the field of biotechnology. In its current state of development, academic biotechnology research can create intellectual property of commercial value without a large research gap between the product concept and the technology that will realize a commercial application. Of course there is a huge gap between identification of an interesting technology and its appearance in the marketplace. The government requirements for proof of efficacy and safety can take years. But this work is entirely within the pharmaceutical firm sponsoring the university's research. Thus, in effect, the pharmaceutical firm minimizes the culture gap by using its own sophisticated research staff, whose scientific credentials are comparable with those of most university biologists, as the interface with the university.

At the risk of oversimplification, there are two ways to reduce the information and trust gap between firm and university: Either the firm uses its corporate research laboratory as the interface, extending the firm's role into the sphere of academic science, or the university finds the financing (either its own, as discussed in

Chapter III, or the state or federal government's, as we shall see in a moment) to reduce the faculty's science to a technology more nearly ready for commercial application.

The Limits of Strategy: Barriers to Early-Stage Technology-Based Innovation

Innovators respond to economic incentives as well as pride of accomplishment. They are well aware of the skewness of returns from investments in science-based innovation—evidence for which is provided in the following contributed chapter by Scherer and Harhoff. Some may well be motivated by the lure of very large (if unlikely and long deferred) returns. Others may be discouraged by the higher likelihood of modest or negative returns. In any case both are dependent on sources of capital that are more conservative in estimates of likely payback, are aware that skewness in returns makes portfolio investment strategies problematical, and are aware of the imperfect appropriability of returns from research expenditures.

Entrepreneurs are, by definition, those who rate their chances of success highly—those who don't, do not become entrepreneurs. The greater the skewness of returns, the greater the observed difference in behavior between those rate their chances of success highly and those who do not. In this sense, skewness of returns—while a deterrent to all those who are intimidated by risk—works to shift the balance of effort in favor of those who embrace uncertainty (with greater concern for upside benefit than downside risk). In this sense (to paraphrase from Schumpeter) large prizes are needed to call forth the effort of the many required for the success of the few.

Normal business case solutions will undervalue upside potential, if only because "net present value" methods do not value the information acquired in the process of the research projects, which creates new options for the firm. A full valuation would include not only the net present value of the innovation in question, but also the value of the options created (see Amram and Kulatilaka 1999). But even if such calculations are more or less correct, and entrepreneurs and their investors can overcome the economic realities of limited appropriability of R&D expenditures, the skewness of returns and the unquantifiable uncertainties of success, institutional "gap" issues which are the focus of this book, may obstruct the development of the innovation by creating additional barriers unrelated to the inherent promise of the technology/product.

We began this book with the proposal that moving from invention to innovation means successfully bridging three institutional and behavioral "gaps": a financing gap between research funds for idea creation and investment funds for idea commercialization; a research gap between an inquiry guided by scientists' judgment of "interestingness" and a product development process guided by market needs; and a trust/information gap between the technologist who knows the science and the investor/manager who knows the business. We then examined the relationship between technical and market risk, the characteristics of the private institutions involved in overcoming technical risk, and the different approaches to technical uncertainty taken by firms of different size and scope. We also described how some publicly funded institutions—primarily universities—are integrated into the private innovation system. In Chapter V we return to our opening theme, taking a further look at barriers to early-stage, technology-based innovation with particular attention to the appropriate role of government in helping to overcome those barriers.

Notes

1. Portfolio strategies rely on a cluster of investments sufficiently large and diverse that a few winners with returns far above average might more than compensate for the moderate or negative returns of the others.

2. In the jargon of academic economics, above-normal profits of this variety are sometimes referred to as "quasi-rents." The prefix "quasi-" suggests the transitory nature of the returns to innovation, in contrast to the rather more permanent nature of rents from fundamentally fixed factors such as land.

3. We thank Robert Frosch for guiding us to this direct expression of the problem.

4. In the paper these are termed Monte Carlo experiments. "Monte Carlo" here refers to a simulation technique (for a description see Judd 1998: Chapter 8).

5. Kenneth Morse, director of MIT's Entrepreneurship Center, notes that portfolio strategies may have the further undesirable effect of making top management relax. He cited as an example Wave Division Multiplex technology,

which was developing slowly at AT&T. Venture capitalists and MIT observed this pace of development and concluded that "Lucent is asleep." They decided to move quickly. Three competitor companies on Route 128 pushed AT&T into moving faster and succeeding. Competitive challenge can be a great stimulus to technical progress.

6. This section was written by Michael J. Roberts, Executive Director of Entrepreneurial Studies, Harvard Business School, and is drawn directly from Branscomb, Morse, and Roberts (2000).

7. The value chain comprises all the elements of a sale that contribute to customer satisfaction and value, which may go far beyond function, quality, and price of the product, to include service, parts supply, training in use, environmental acceptability, user safety, trusted relationship with the vendor, and so on.

8. McGroddy illustrates with the example of routers: IBM built the backbone of the Internet, but McGroddy could not convince IBM top management to get into the router business. The perceived problem was that IBM routers would have competed with established IBM business in SNA controllers. Two years later Cisco, which now dominates the router market, had half of IBM's market capitalization; it now exceeds IBM's market capitalization.

9. McGroddy cites the example of IBM-owned laser business in Zurich that earned $150 million profit over six years before being sold.

10. The idea of "trickle-up" strategy for introducing new technology is the result of an unpublished contract study made for IBM in about 1984 of the way the top dozen consumer electronic firms in the world (Philips and 11 Japanese firms) managed their technology strategies.

11. The role of university consultants to firms is important for another reason. A study of IBM's extensive research contracts with universities in the mid 1980s (about $73 million in annual value) showed that the event that led most frequently to a contract was the hiring of the lead faculty member as a consultant to address some problem of technical difficulty. (Branscomb 1986).

Technology Policy for a World of Skew-Distributed Outcomes

F. M. Scherer and Dietmar Harhoff

During the past several years the authors have been compiling data on the size distribution of financial returns within samples of significant technological innovations. Our uniform finding is that the returns are skew-distributed. Most innovations yield modest returns, but the size distribution has a long thin tail encompassing a relatively few innovations with particularly high returns. In this essay, we review earlier research, summarize our new evidence, and suggest implications for technology policy.

1. Prior Research

Until recently there has been relatively little systematic empirical research on the statistical distribution properties of the returns from invention and innovation. Drawing upon a small sample survey of U.S. patents, Scherer (1965: 1098) discovered a distribution of estimated profits from patented inventions so skew that "patent statistics are likely to measure run-of-the-mill industrial inventive output much more accurately than they reflect the occasional strategic inventions which open up new markets and new technologies. The latter must probably remain the domain of economic historians." A second line of investigation differentiated the value of patents by the time their holders chose not to pay the annual renewal fees imposed in some nations. The pioneering article in this tradition, overlooked by subsequent investigators, was by Dernburg and Gharrity (1961–1962). Leading examples of later investigations using more powerful econometric techniques include Pakes and Schankerman (1984), Pakes (1986), Schankerman and Pakes (1986), and Lanjouw, Pakes, and Putnam (1996). These studies confirmed that the size distribution of patent values is indeed quite skew, most likely conforming either to a log normal or a Paretian distribution law. A third line of research by Grabowski and Vernon (1990, 1994) used the particularly rich data available on sales of individual ethical drugs throughout the world to estimate the distribution of profits or, more exactly, quasi-rents attained by samples of new drugs approved by the U.S. Food and Drug Administration (FDA). Again, a skew distribution was found, leading inter alia to the conclusion that heavy-handed price controls could jeopardize the continued vitality of new drug discovery and testing efforts (see, e.g., Grabowski and Vernon, 1996; Scherer, 1996).

2. The New Evidence

Altogether, we have assembled eight data sets, seven of which are new to the literature. Table 1 describes the samples and provides a simple indicator of distribution skewness–the fraction of total sample profits, royalties, or stock market value contributed by the 10% of the sample members realizing the highest absolute or relative rewards. In the most ambitious of our efforts, we collected survey and interview evidence on 772 German- and 222 U.S.-origin inventions, on all of which German patent applications were filed in 1977, leading to issued German patents considered sufficiently valuable by their holders to warrant paying annual renewal fees totalling DM 16,075 until their expiration at full term in 1995. These are called the "German patents" and "U.S. patents" in Table 1.[1] Figure 1 shows the distribution of summed German patent values by value class intervals, with the number of patents in each value category given in parentheses above the bars. Fifty-four percent of the value is concentrated in the five inventions with values of DM 50 million or more.

Our first-stage patent survey methodology asked company respondents to answer a single counter-factual question, phrased as follows in the U.S. survey:

Technology Policy and Skew-Distributed Outcomes

Table 1 Proportion of innovation samples' total value realized by the most valuable 10% of innovations

Data set	Number of observations	Percent of value in top 10%
German patents	772	84
U.S. patents	222	81–85
Harvard patents	118	84
Six university patents		
1991 royalties	350	93
1992 royalties	408	92
1993 royalties	466	91.5
1994 royalties	411	92
Venture Economics start-ups	383	62
Horseley-Keogh start-ups	670	59
Initial public stock offerings (1995 stock values of 1983–85 IPOs)	110	62
Grabowski-Vernon		
1970s drugs	98	55
1980s drugs	66	48

If in 1980 you knew what you now know about the profit history of the invention abstracted here, what is the smallest amount for which you would have been willing to sell this patent to an independent third party, assuming that you had a bona fide offer to purchase and that the buyer would subsequently exercise its full patent rights?

In the first-stage survey, respondents were asked to place each sample patent in one of five value categories ranging from less than DM 40,000 to more than DM 5 million. Fifty-six on-site interviews were held with companies reporting patents valued at more than DM 5 million, making it possible to elicit more detailed discounted profitability and invention value estimates. Because selling full rights meant that the patent holder could be enjoined from using its invention or forced to pay royalties reflecting the invention's value, the survey responses elicited private value estimates (grouped in value class intervals) corresponding most closely to the dis-

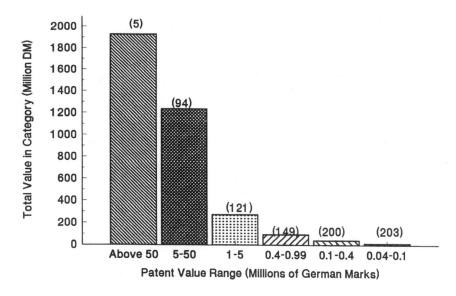

Figure 1 Distribution of German patent values.

counted present value of profits that would be foregone by not having the invention and its accompanying patent protection. As such, the estimates are roughly two orders of magnitude higher than those obtained in statistical studies of patent renewal, which implicitly assess only the value of patent protection, given disclosure and non-patent barriers to imitation, not the value of the invention per se, and which estimate the value of the presumptively most valuable full-term patents only by extrapolation.

Two other data sets also focused on invention patents, one tallying the royalties received between 1977 and 1995 on 118 patent "bundles" covering inventions made by Harvard University employees and licensed by the Harvard Office of Technology Licensing, the other analogous royalties received during the years 1991 through 1994 on inventions made at six research-oriented U.S. universities. These are called the "Harvard patents" and "six university patents" in Table 1. The "Venture Economics start-ups" and "Horsley-Keogh start-ups" samples in Table 1 evaluated the asset value appreciation (or loss) experienced on a total of 1053 investments in start-up companies by U.S. venture capital firms between

1969 and 1988. The "IPOs" sample measures the appreciation of common stock values as of 1995 for 110 high-technology companies that made IPOs between 1983 and 1985. Finally, we take advantage of the data compiled and analyzed previously by Grabowski and Vernon (1990, 1994) on the discounted present value of quasi-rents realized on new pharmaceutical entities marketed in the United States–98 of them introduced during the 1970s and 66 between 1980 and 1984.

In all cases, a relatively small number of top entities were responsible for most of the total value realized from the full cohort of innovations. The highest concentration of value is found for the patents, which tend to cover the narrowest range of innovative subject matter. The fraction of total portfolio value attributable to the top 10% of start-up business investments is quite similar for the two sets of venture fund-backed companies and for the IPO companies (whose value gains occur at a later life cycle stage, since venture funds typically liquidate their positions shortly after the companies they have backed float IPOs). The least skewness is found for the new drug entity samples, perhaps in part because the samples include only products that had passed through rigorous FDA approval regimens. For the German patents, Harvard patents, IPOs, and Grabowski-Vernon drug products, the data were of sufficient richness that we could statistically test alternative distribution form hypotheses (see Harhoff et al. 1997, Scherer 1998, and Scherer, Harhoff, and Kukies 1999). For all five samples, the best-fitting distribution was the log normal (surpassing, e.g., Pareto-Levy, Weibull, negative exponential, and Maddala-Singh alternatives). The Grabowski-Vernon drug distributions, with the lowest fraction of value residing in the most valuable 10% of observations, were discernibly less skew than the log normal, but clearly more skew than alternatives such as the Weibull. This finding will be important at a subsequent stage of the argument.

3. Implications for R&D Funding Agencies

Our research reveals that the lion's share of the privately appropriated value through investments in innovation comes from roughly 10% of the technically successful prospects. This is true for patents, which typically cover quite narrow slices of technology, for discrete products (e.g., new drug chemical entities), and for whole firms securing venture capital or new public issue financing. Our study of high-technology start-up firms' stock market performance over roughly 10 years reveals in addition that it is difficult to predict in advance which of the prospects considered attractive enough to warrant investment will pay off most lucratively.

A further, less fully documented, step must be taken to draw implications for technology policy, as implemented by governmental organizations. None of our data sets attempted to measure the social returns realized through technological innovation. However, there is no reason to suppose that the size distribution of payoffs from government research and/or development projects is qualitatively different from what we have observed for our samples of private sector and university projects. Fragmentary evidence suggests that the social returns from private investments and the returns from government projects are similarly skew-distributed. Thus, one cannot reject even at the 20% confidence level the hypothesis that the social rates of return calculated by Mansfield et al. (1977) on 16 private-sector innovations were log-normally distributed.[2] Similarly, crude data on the number of combat vehicles produced following government R&D programs in the fighter aircraft, bomber, and guided missile fields reveal a skew distribution.[3] Thus, for the inferences made in the next two paragraphs, we assume that the size distributions of returns from government projects have skewness properties similar to those we have observed in our more thoroughly analyzed private sector data sets.

Legislators and senior government leaders are likely to view government technology programs in which half the supported projects fail to yield appreciable returns and only one in 10 succeeds handsomely as a rather poor track record when in fact, by the standards of private sector markets, it is quite normal.[4] Those who are responsible for the allocation of financial resources to support the advance of technology should adjust their expectations accordingly. Similarly, researchers who seek to assess the success of government technology programs should focus most of their effort on measuring returns from the relatively few projects with clearly superior payoffs, not on projects in the heavily populated low-value distribution tail.

Our results also suggest the wisdom for technology policy in Mao Tse-Tung's aphorism, "Let one hundred flowers bloom"–implemented, to be sure, with greater discrimination and consistency than Chairman Mao exhibited in his Great Leap Forward. Among other things, technology policies that concentrate government subsidies on a relatively few national champion enterprises may fail through insufficient statistical diversity, even if (as is debatable) leading firms embrace new technological opportunities as enthusiastically as their smaller counterparts.[5] Rather, from our findings one gains enhanced appreciation of the U.S. venture funding system, under which private risk capital flows each year to thousands of high-technology start-up companies in the hope that the returns from a handful will compensate, or more than compensate, the investors. Most industrialized nations have been slow in imitating that institution, which was almost surely the principal basis of U.S. success in high-technology industries during the past decade.[6]

4. The Efficacy of Portfolio Strategies

All this suggests the need for both nations and firms to pursue a portfolio approach to backing new technology, recognizing that only a few of the projects supported will pay off on a large scale and hoping that generous returns from the relatively few successes will cover the cost of the many less successful projects. One should not, however, exaggerate the efficacy of portfolio strategies as a means of hedging against the risks from investing in new technologies.

We began our research hypothesizing provisionally, based upon fragmentary earlier evidence, that the returns from investments in new technology adhered to a Pareto-Levy distribution. If V is the value of profits from an innovation, N is the number of cases with value V or greater, and k and a are positive parameters, the simplest Pareto-Levy distribution is characterized by the equation

$$N(V) = k V - a .$$

This equation is linear in the logarithms, with a long thin tail into the highest-value range of innovation profits. The Pareto-Levy distribution has the unusual property that when $a = 1$, the weak law of large numbers fails to hold, so that neither the distribution's mean nor its variance is asymptotically finite. What this means in practical terms is that as one draws ever larger samples, there is an increasing probability that some extremely large observation will materialize, causing both the mean and the variance to explode upward rather than converging toward stable values. This in turn implies that it is difficult or impossible to achieve stable mean expectations and hence hedge against risk by supporting sizeable portfolios of projects.

Our research failed for the most part to support the Paretian hypothesis, pointing instead toward log normal distributions with better-behaved large-sample properties. That is good news for the users of portfolio strategies. However, the log normal distributions we observed were themselves quite skew and indeed hard to distinguish statistically in their extreme-value tails from Paretian distributions. This suggests that attempts to achieve stable mean returns through feasible portfolio strategies are likely to yield at best middling success.

To demonstrate this point, we report on a series of Monte Carlo experiments using the Grabowski-Vernon quasi-rent data for 98 new drugs that cleared FDA regulatory hurdles and were intro- duced into the U.S. market during the 1970s. The distribution of 1970s drug quasi-rents, we recall from Table 1, was the second-to- least skew of any of the distributions on which we obtained data, and thus it provides a relatively optimistic test of the problems that attend portfolio strategies.

Each individual quasi-rent observation in the Grabowski-Vernon data set was replicated 10 times, and the observations were stored in a (figurative) computer urn, where their order was randomized. From supplementary data that underlay the Grabowski-Vernon quasi-rent estimates, it was assumed that the typical drug has a rent-earning life of 21 years following its introduction into the market. The rents for any given drug were assumed to be distributed triangularly over time, with peak rent-earning at year 10. During the period for which the Grabowski-Vernon data were collected, an average of 18 new drug chemical entities per year were approved by the FDA and introduced into the U.S. market. Thus, for each year over a total of 70 years, 18 new drugs were drawn randomly from the computer urn. For each drug so drawn, its quasi-rents were spread over 21 years. When the sampling was completed, the quasi-rents of

Technology Policy and Skew-Distributed Outcomes

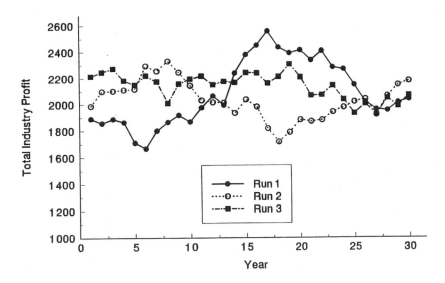

Figure 2 Plot of drug industry profit simulations, runs 1, 2, and 3.

all drugs on the market in any given year (i.e., 18 drugs per year times 21 years = 378 rent-earning drugs) were summed. Because they included incomplete numbers of drugs, the totals for the first and last 20 years were deleted from the sample, leaving quasi-rent totals for 30 years, each year's total comprising the moving sum of 378 observations. After further randomizations, the experiment was repeated over a total of seven complete runs.

The results are summarized in Figures 2 and 3. For all years and all simulations combined, mean annual quasi-rents amounted to US$2.07 billion. Total quasi-rents varied widely from year to year, however, from a minimum of US$1.55 billion (in run 7) to a maximum of US$2.57 billion (in run 5), with an average year-to-year standard deviation of US$168 million. Inspecting any given run's quasi-rent fluctuations without knowing that they were generated by a random sampling process, one might infer that they reveal systematic "cycles" quite like the cycles actually observed in total U.S. drug industry profitability. But this would be wrong. Rather, the year-to-year and sample-to-sample variability is typical of what happens when one draws relatively large samples of individual values that are skew-distributed.

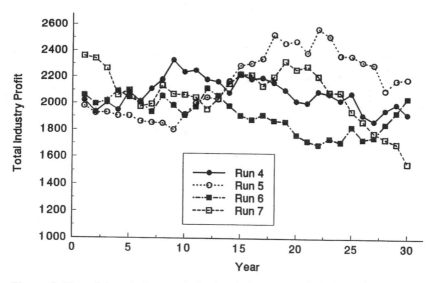

Figure 3 Plot of drug industry profit simulations, runs 4, 5, 6 and 7.

The annual quasi-rent totals presented in Figures 2 and 3 stem from a methodology that in effect covers all the new products on the U.S. market in any given year over the products' life cycles. Thus, they reflect portfolio averaging at the whole pharmaceutical industry level. Even with a skew log normal distribution, it remains true that the more observations over which one samples, the more stable the year-to-year averages (or totals) are. Thus, recent mergers among pharmaceutical companies, motivated in part by a desire to create larger portfolios spreading the risks of individual R&D project investments, undoubtedly do reduce the year-to-year variability of outcomes. But even at the extreme of merging the entire industry into one hypothetical firm, year-to-year standard deviations equal to roughly 8% of industry quasi-rent totals remain. For individual firms much smaller than the pharmaceutical industry aggregate, substantially larger year-to-year variations cannot be escaped through portfolio strategies.[7] Thus, given skew-distributed outcomes, appreciable risk-taking cannot be avoided. And in judging the innovative performance of individual firms, a long time perspective is essential, since short-run returns can be dominated by particularly favorable or unfavorable draws from a skew distribution.

5. Macroeconomic Implications

Recall that the drug quasi-rent distribution used as the basis for our Monte Carlo analysis was less skew than all but one of the distributions summarized in Table 1. For the other, more skew distributions, one would expect even more instability of means and totals for relatively large samples–e.g., extending to the whole-industry level. This raises a question: Might the skewness of innovation outcome distributions contribute instability even when the individual effects are aggregated up to the level of a whole economy? In other words, might the real business cycles (more accurately, business fluctuations) to which macroeconomists have called attention be attributable in part to randomness in draws from a skew-distributed universe of innovative opportunities? A Monte Carlo experiment by Nordhaus (1989) suggests that they may be. He postulated that 99.99% of the tens of thousands of invention patents issued each year are worthless, but that the remaining 0.01% (three to eight inventions per year) have high values adhering to a Pareto distribution with a fairly conservative a coefficient of 1.3. The effects of those valuable inventions were assumed to seep into the economy slowly but persist indefinitely. Making random draws from his Pareto distribution and aggregating the effects, Nordhaus simulated year-to-year fluctuations in economy-wide productivity growth ranging from 0.5% to 3.5% per year in a seemingly cyclical pattern resembling the productivity growth fluctuations actually experienced by the U.S. economy over the years 1900 through 1988.

We had contemplated performing a similar analysis using our much richer data, but concluded that the additional assumptions required would overwhelm the empirical observations and therefore that the results would be too assumption-dependent to provide reliable insights. There were three problem clusters.

First, our data are uniformly for private economic values, whereas a proper macroeconomic analysis requires the use of social returns to innovation, taking into account unappropriated benefits and other externalities, not merely private returns. The translation from private to social returns must have large but poorly understood stochastic components.[8]

Second, our patented invention samples are limited to a single year's cohort, and hence may not have captured the most extreme private values. And for the U.S. sample, the survey elicited value estimates only for discrete categories, including an open-ended category of US$100 million and more. We know from telephone interviews with respondents that some of the 18 estimates in the highest category were valued at more than US$1 billion, but the evidence is too incomplete to support a confident extrapolation. Assuming the categorical data to be Pareto-distributed and extrapolating linearly from the fitted U.S. patent size distribution to the extreme tail, one finds the most valuable invention in our sample to have a private value of US$90 billion (see Harhoff, Scherer, and Vopel 1997). But given the more complete evidence from other samples, it is unlikely that the log linearity associated with a Pareto distribution persists into the extreme tail, and so the validity of this extrapolation is dubious.[9] If one ignores that hazard, crude simulations imposing minimal structure on the data reveal sufficient skewness to generate macroeconomic fluctuations of appreciable magnitude.

Third, too little is known about the detailed structure of individual innovations' macroeconomic effects. For any given innovation value, longer lag structures will produce smoother effects than short lags; Koyck-type lags will impart sharper fluctuations than, e.g., lag effects distributed in a bell-curve pattern over time.[10] Major innovations can generate positive multiplier effects, and reverse causality can also intrude as macroeconomic swings induce demand-pull effects on the supply of innovations (see Schmookler 1966). Interactions among individual inventions also cannot be ignored. Simulation analyses suggest, for example, that both complementarities and competitive interactions among inventions with Pareto-distributed individual values lead to revised value distributions that are less skew than Pareto.

Given these difficulties, we chose not to attempt a full-scale Monte Carlo analysis of macroeconomic implications. The most that can be said is that the skew distribution of innovation values could in principle lead to noticeable macroeconomic fluctuations, and that must remain a tantalizing hypothesis for future research.

6. Conclusions

Our empirical research reveals at a high level of confidence that the size distribution of private value returns from individual technological innovations is quite skew—most likely adhering to a log normal law. A small minority of innovations yield the lion's share of all innovations' total economic value. This implies difficulty in averting risk through portfolio strategies and in assessing individual organizations' innovation track records. Assuming similar degrees of skewness in the returns from projects undertaken under government sponsorship, public sector programs seeking to support major technological advances must strive to let many flowers bloom. The skewness of innovation returns almost surely persists to add instability to the profit returns of whole industries and may extend even up to the macroeconomic level. Although much remains to be learned, some important lessons for technology policy have begun to emerge.

Acknowledgments

This essay is reprinted from *Research Policy* 29 (4-5): 559–566, a special issue on The Economics of Technology Policy, edited by Albert Link and David Roessner, ©2000 Elsevier Science. See <www.elsevier.com/homepage/sae/econbase/respol/menu.sht>. Financial support from the Sloan Foundation and the Mannheim, Germany, Center for European Economic Research at earlier stages of this project is gratefully acknowledged.

Notes

1. A detailed analysis may be found in Harhoff, Scherer, and Vopel (1997). The monetary patent value estimates are linked to subsequent patent citations in Harhoff et al. (1999).

2. One negative observation was excluded, leaving 16 useable observations, whose distribution in the logarithms had a skewness coefficient of 0.05 and a kurtosis coefficient of 2.53. The values for a perfect log normal distribution would be 0 and 3.0, respectively. For the 16 observations before logarithmic transformation, the skewness coefficient was 1.83, which differs from normality at the 0.01 significance level. Mansfield et al. (1977) estimated internal rates of return rather than undiscounted or discounted total returns, as in our samples. The distributions of internal rates of return are intrinsically less skew than

present values of absolute payoffs, calculated at conventional discount rates,. because the polynomial deflation carried out to determine internal rates of return tends to suppress very large values.

3. These estimates were made by co-author Scherer in work done for the U.S. Department of Justice in opposition to a merger between Lockheed-Martin and Northrop-Grumman.

4. We owe this insight to Arati Prabhakar, former director of DARPA and then the U.S. National Institute of Standards and Technology, from a discussion at a U.S. Department of Defense Science Council meeting in 1993.

5. Compare Scherer (1992) and Christensen (1997).

6. For a comparative analysis of various leading nations' high-technology venture systems, see U.S. National Science Board (1998: 6–33). For a comparison of U.S. and German systems, see Kukies and Scherer (1998).

7. Thus, for a drug firm one-fifth the size of the total industry, the year-to-year standard deviation (assuming log normality) would be on the order of 18%; for a firm one-tenth the size of the industry, approximately 25%.

8. The most relevant analysis, focusing on internal rates of return rather than absolute magnitudes, is by Mansfield et al. (1977). The simple (Piersonian) correlation between their social and private rate of return estimates for 17 innovations was +0.47.

9. To be sure, innovations with social payoffs of that magnitude (e.g., 3.2% of 1980 U.S. GDP) undoubtedly exist. Probable examples include Alexander Graham Bell's telephone, Edison's electric light (Nordhaus 1997), the Otto internal combustion engine, television, integrated circuits and microprocessors, and the Cohen-Boyer gene splicing inventions (whose three patents are included in our six universities sample, yielding US$75 million in royalties from numerous non-exclusive licenses during 1991–1994). Most of these innovations were covered by multiple patents, some competing and some complementary.

10. See e.g., Ravenscraft and Scherer (1982).

V

Overcoming Barriers

The goal of technology policy is not to substitute the government's judgment for that of private industry in deciding which potential "winners" to back. Rather, the point is to correct market failure.
—President Bill Clinton, *1994 Economic Report of the President*

The numerous "market failures" commonly invoked in defense of an active federal technology policy have been exhaustively studied by economists and policy analysts. All are based to some extent or another on the inability of firms to capture the full benefits of the innovations they create.[1] The evidence is indeed strong that, from the perspective of societal benefits, commercial firms have inadequate incentives to undertake high-risk technology development projects.[2] Yet imperfect appropriability of returns from innovation has *not* been the focus of our narrative. Instead, we have argued that *institutions for innovation* are as important as *returns from* innovation. In any given setting, managers and investors make the best decisions they can in the interest of their own firms, balancing investment, risk, and opportunity for return. Economic arguments that individual firms may underinvest in innovation from the perspective of public returns provide the *motivation* for federal and state activities to encourage it. Indeed, the variety of other sources of discouragement we have listed, both economic and structural, suggest that the appropriability arguments probably underestimate the difference between the returns to society and to the firm. The *mechanisms* for lowering institutional barriers to innovation, discussed here, can increase returns to both the individual firm and the economy as a whole.

Technology-Based Innovation: Institutional Requirements

As we noted earlier, there a few ways to succeed but many ways to fail in science-based innovations. Among the requirements for success noted by both managers and investors in our workshops are these:

• *A technical team that is sufficiently prepared* for the inevitable surprises with which nature challenges innovators, for lack of critical technical information, the necessary skills and experience, or access to help from consultants or other collaborating firms or universities. The precise scope of the required technical knowledge is often unknown in advance. This puts a premium on the depth and breadth of the accessible scientific and technological information, and the skill to look outside the firm to acquire it.

• *A champion* who not only believes in the idea of the innovation, but can earn the trust of investors and create an affordable business environment within which the idea can be nurtured. As Mark Chalek of Boston's Beth Israel Deaconess Medical Center observes: "What typically impedes our technology from becoming commercialized is [the absence of] some mitigating, facilitating entity— whether you want to call it an incubator, whether you want to call it a group of facilitators, or group of managers, or all of the above— who have the ability to both validate the technology from a commercial perspective and take it to that next stage which includes getting it ready for financing and also getting it ready for commercialization."

• *A flexible business management,* if the innovation is to be pursued in an existing firm, that sees opportunity in the innovation rather than competition for the firm's existing business. Steve Kent, Chief Scientist of BBN Systems and Technologies, observed that BBN had an experience similar to that of IBM with respect to the Internet router market (see the contributed essay by McGroddy). Routers competed with BBN's successful X25 packet business. The entire marketing organization—which had an important say in how research money would be spent—argued there was no future in routers. This was no surprise, as BBN's customers were exactly those people who wanted to buy X25 packets.

• *Early and accurate information from the market.* This is the primary argument of David Lewis of Lord Corporation, who stresses that detailed knowledge of the market substantially reduces the technical risk of failing to meet the required specifications. Similarly, James McGroddy notes that in its core business (computers) IBM was able to take great technical risks, but, as Branscomb reports, this was not the case outside the core when IBM attempted to incubate new businesses in unfamiliar markets such as medical and scientific instruments.

• *Technical specifications* derived from a clearly defined business model. The business model maps technical inputs to economic outputs. As Chesbrough and Rosenbloom remind us in their contributed essay, the business model identifies the market segments, articulates the value proposition, defines the structure of the value chain, estimates the cost structure and profit potential, positions the firm within the value network, and formulates a competitive strategy in the prospective marketplace. This is the context which the product specifications must satisfy, placing a severe burden on the technology as it develops.

• *A source of seed financing* to facilitate the conversion of concepts to the point where venture and debt capital might be available. This is a traditional role for "angel" investors. Those who became wealthy by creating successful, innovative businesses can bring experience as well as finance to a new venture. But there is an increasing opportunity for government research funding here, in part because much of the growth in new venture formation stems from government-funded research, either indirectly through research support in universities and national laboratories or directly through federal programs like ATP and SBIR or state-funded innovation programs.

• *A network of relationships* that help an emergent firm to avoid errors and, more importantly, save precious time. The main lesson of the two cases discussed earlier, AIR and Trexel, was the vital importance of a network of expertise in research, technology development, management, and investment. But equally important is the availability of a responsive financial and service infrastructure in the community, familiar with the requirements and styles of work of the emerging industry. It is these services that largely determine the economic success of concentrations of innovative firms in places like Silicon Valley and Route 128.

The absence of any of these requirements constitutes a barrier to innovation. The next question is, can Federal or state agencies help ensure their presence?

Government Sources of Support for Technical Risk Mitigation

Both federal and state governments recognize, at least in principle, that there are institutional and financial barriers to innovation that government action might help to reduce. Certainly the federal role is most self-evident in helping firms meet the first requirement: the availability of the technical knowledge and skill base. Since the federal government sponsors half of the basic research and a third of all research and development in the nation, the question becomes: Can a federal agency such as the National Institute for Standards and Technology (NIST) determine the areas of research that are most responsive to the needs of innovators and create relationships and networks with and among firms that will ensure the diffusion of the knowledge into the economy?

At the state level the motivation for promoting innovation is clear: Increase employment demand and per capita income in the state, at the expense of other states if necessary. At the federal level the motivation comes more from a desire to exploit the enormous federal investment in research and development for economic purposes. In 1998 total R&D expenditures in the United States reached $227.2 billion, of which $66.9 billion came from federal appropriations. But since most of the private R&D investment was for development, it is more relevant for our purposes to compare research investments. Here the federal government's share is much larger. For the sum of basic and applied research, NSF estimates that government spent $34.561 billion and industry $44.938 billion in 1998 (U. S. National Science Board 2000: Tables 2–9, 2–13). In basic research the government outspent industry almost 2:1 ($20.2 billion vs. $11.3

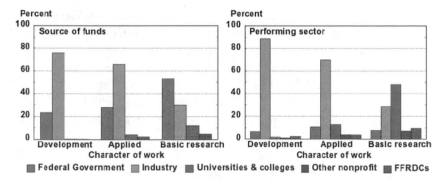

Figure V-1 National R&D expenditures, by source of funds, performing sector, and character of work: 1998. Source: U.S. National Science Board (2000: 2–31).

billion). This is the rich load of new technical knowledge from which innovations may spring. See Figure V-1.

Thus it is reasonable for the federal government to look for ways to extract more public benefit from its basic research investments. One way to do this is to sponsor research in firms that advances technical knowledge of strategic value, while helping the firm reduce its technical risks.

State-Financed Programs to Promote Innovation

State-funded programs for promoting innovation within the state are clearly intended to compensate for geographical concentration, or, more specifically, to create jobs and income for the state by nurturing new firms or attracting them from other states. Since most of their strategies emphasize "high-tech" industry, hoping to compensate for declines in more traditional areas such as agriculture, steel, or extractive industries, these programs provide a possible source of assistance in reducing technical risks or compensating forms for enduring them.

In fiscal year 1995 state-funded cooperative technology programs increased to $405 million. This total reflects only those programs administered by state governments, supporting government-industry or government-industry-university partnerships with the primary goal of using technology to promote economic growth. At this time the states seem to be accelerating their interest in this effort to stimulate innovation. In the period 1992–1995 Arizona's budget increased seven-fold, Wisconsin's more than quadrupled, and Kentucky's budget doubled (State Science and Technology Institute 1996). State spending on R&D, most of which was spent in universities, totaled $2.431 billion in 1995 (U. S. National Science Board 2000: text table 2-7). These assets may be available to firms seeking to reduce their financial exposure to risk or seeking access to scientific resources that can mitigate risks.

Federal R&D Programs to Promote Innovation

Unlike the states, which are politically quite comfortable competing with one another to attract new business through active programs of R&D subsidies, federal politics views with suspicion government programs to assist individual firms. There are three major exceptions to this generalization, however: (a) where the government is the consumer of the ultimate products (notably defense equipment), (b) where there is a major government mission dependent on industrial innovation (such as health, environment, or safety) or (c) for programs such as those supporting small businesses that are designed to be so politically attractive that theoretical and ideological objections carry little weight. Until recently the federal government financed the majority of research performed in the United States. Private funding has been rising more quickly during the healthy economic growth of the late 1990s, while federal research expenditures have been held nearly constant for the last decade. Thus the federal share of R&D funding in the United States has fallen from 67 percent in 1964, to 47 percent in 1988, to 29.5 percent in 1998, the lowest ever recorded in the National Science Foundation's data series (U. S. National Science Board 2000: 2–10). Health-related research has been growing, while defense research has declined. With the political saliency of economic and physical health overtaking that of national security, Congress has adopted a broad range of policies intended to link government-funded research to the promotion of commercial innovation (Branscomb and Keller 1998).

One example is the Advanced Technology Program (ATP) within the National Institute of Standards and Technology of the U.S.

Department of Commerce. The Congress views the ATP as a form of public-private partnership, in which a government agency, NIST, promotes economic growth by sharing the cost of early stage research in new or existing firms (Hill 1998: 143–173). This ATP research is intended to develop innovative technologies that, despite being high in technical risk, are "enabling" in the sense of having the potential to provide significant, broad-based benefits.

Since its inception in 1990, the ATP has successfully completed 40 competitions involving over 1,067 project participants and resulting in 468 awards to single companies and joint ventures. The ATP has awarded approximately $1,496 million, and industry has provided approximately $1,499 million in matching funds.[3] Public officials characterize the selection criteria for research undertaken in ATP projects as "high risk." The question of whether high risk is a positive attribute of radical, science-based innovations or rather should be seen as a negative characteristic is a central one in the ATP project selection process. Venture capitalists rarely see technical risk as a positive; some R&D managers use the term to imply that a project has more than the usual uncertainties as to outcomes, which may nevertheless be justified because it has higher than normal prospects for "destabilizing" a market, that is, for disrupting an old market and replacing it with a new one, a position that can be protected through exclusive ownership of intellectual property.

The program's mission is to "assist United States businesses in creating and applying generic technology and research results necessary to: (1) commercialize significant new scientific discoveries and technologies rapidly; and (2) refine manufacturing technologies … giving preference to technologies that have great economic potential."[4] Industry proposes research projects to ATP in fair, rigorous competitions, in which projects are selected for funding based on both their technical and their economic and business merit.

The ATP program was accessible from the beginning to both individual firms and consortia of firms eager to share a new technology if it could be made practical. In 1993 the Clinton administration introduced an innovation: ATP would invite industries to propose "focus areas" for ATP investment. The idea was to produce more measurable economic effects and encourage technology diffusion by concentrating $ 30 to 40 million in each of several industrial technology areas. The grants themselves could be to individual firms or to groups of firms, but all would be aware of the common target area for research. This approach seemed attractive to most observers, but was terminated by ATP management in response to objections to it from the U.S. Senate.

The role of universities in ATP is defined in the statute. Universities can participate in the consortia of firms proposing projects to ATP, but they cannot serve as the project leader (prime contractor). A significant fraction of ATP funding flows to university laboratories acting as joint venture partners of the firms, and in many cases the experts in the universities have also served as advisors to the firms creating the proposal, thus strongly influencing the technical goals and strategies. Universities have often sought the opportunity to act as prime contractors for ATP group projects; however, this would require a change in the legislation and would probably be opposed by the administration.

The decision to establish the ATP was based on three premises. The first is that, under certain circumstances, firms and investors may see insufficient market incentives to fund development projects that involve a high degree of new technical content and that therefore have high outcome uncertainties. However, for promising technologies, the probability of returns to the economy as a whole might fully justify the investment. When this is the case, and the expected social return is sufficiently high, it may be in the national interest for the government to support the development of such potentially neglected projects.

The second premise is that with the above justification for federal investments in science-based innovations, government agencies can, in fact, define and manage programs of cost-shared investment which are economically effective, manageable, and politically acceptable.

The third premise is that programs like ATP need only be modestly efficient to leverage the economic value of the $34.561 billion in basic and applied research the federal government funded in 1998 and more than pay for themselves. There are serious questions about the effectiveness with which the commercial world gains access to the fruits of $30.447 billions of federally sponsored work in universities, national laboratories, and not-for-profits, which provides yet another motivation for government to enhance the diffusion of new science to new markets (Branscomb and Keller 1998). This would seem to be a particularly strong argument when there are clearly apparent gaps—financial, technical, and organizational—between the new commercial concepts born from the $30 billions of government-funded research in nonprofits and the commercial products created by the $182 billion of industrially funded development.

Is the ATP Program Both Justified and Effective?

The bulk of analysis by academics on government support for technology development in general, and ATP in particular, has focused on the issue of social returns—*why* the government should support these programs—and in particular assessing the existence, measurability, and geographical localization of knowledge and market "spillovers" resulting from the success of high-risk technological ventures (Mansfield et al. 1977; Griliches 1992). Far less attention has been paid to *how* government programs can reduce institutional, behavioral, and non-financial barriers to innovation that may inhibit economic actors—entrepreneurs, venture capitalists, or corporations—from undertaking projects with a high degree of inherent technical risk.

The ATP program measures its success by assessing not only technical success or failure in its projects, but also the dissemination of the technical learning and other technical assets (such as intellectual property) to the economy.[5] The primary mechanism for dissemination is successful commercialization. However, ATP also makes an effort to track the flow of technical knowledge (for example, as evidenced by patent citations) from projects that are technical successes but commercial failures.[6] This is important, as valuable technical knowledge may be created in projects that are not immediate business successes. Policy objectives in the area of early-stage, technology-based research would be clarified by a better understanding of the relationship of the commercialization of a technology and the broad dissemination of that technology.

A final question for the public policy maker concerns the widespread agreement among the practitioners that technical risk and product performance are interdependent. ATP evaluates the business case for the technical projects in which it participates. If the process of reduction to practice of the technology entails changes in product performance, the firm can report to its ATP partner the consequent changes in the market segment reached by the project, and thus the business case. Since the ATP uses the "cooperative agreement" form of contract, in which the goals are agreed to by both parties and can by altered by mutual agreement during the course of the project, there is ample flexibility to allow the firm to change its business plan in mid-stream. However, if such changes are incremental and frequent, the required reporting might become an administrative burden on both the firm and the agency. If useful technical knowledge can be disseminated independent of the particular form of first market entry (or even as a result of a "constructive failure"), evaluation criteria should allow considerable flexibility on the specific form of initial economic success, recognizing that markets change and that the results of the technology development itself will inform a company's market strategy.[7]

ATP is seen by the Congress, and by many others, as a very complex program, difficult to describe and defend in a few words. Our conclusion is, however, that the ATP is both effective and justified—effective as evidenced by the extensive analysis that has been performed on the economic returns from completed projects, and justified by the clear evidence that there is a serious market failure represented by the gaps and risk aversion we have described in this book. This does not mean that the effectiveness of the ATP program cannot be improved.

The ATP is aimed squarely at the research and technology gap. It seeks to reduce the technical risks faced by innovators. In the process it helps address the financial gap, since most of the ATP projects are at a stage of technical development that is too immature to attract conventional venture capital investment, or to expect, for reasons we have discussed, much interest from large firms. In many respects it is more deserving of Congressional support than the SBIR program, even though the House of Representatives has more than once voted to terminate ATP and continues to renew and occasionally expand the SBIR.

As we have noted, this disparity is partly the result of a simple fact: SBIR spends far more money than does ATP, without the need for an appropriation, and distributes the money around the country. But more importantly, SBIR is strongly supported by the Small Business Administration and the constituency organizations that represent small business in Washington. What can the ATP do to make itself more attractive to Congress, to improve its political appeal?

First, it should position itself as an R&D program, not an economic development program. It should address the research gap, not the financial gap, even though, as we just noted, in addressing the one it also helps address the other. Its managers should insist that it be evaluated, as DARPA, PNGV, and other technology programs are judged, by the technology produced and by the evidence that this technology is useful for building a more innovative economy. To this end it is necessary to count inventions made, licenses sold, new processes and products designed and produced, and people trained. It should not be necessary to try to measure jobs and wealth created, although the ATP evaluation program has been able to do that.

The ATP should not allow itself to be perceived by academics or congressmen as a "public venture capital" program, for it is not one and could not reasonably accomplish such an assignment. Lerner (2000) has made the reasons for this abundantly clear. It should continue to strengthen its links to state innovation programs and solicit the support of state delegations in its behalf. It should give more prominence to the role of research universities, to the extent that they become important contributors to bridging the research gap. If the opportunity presents itself the Congress should allow universities to initiate and lead ATP consortia involving many firms to pursue meritorious technologies. Finally, it should try to demonstrate that ATP is a modest increment to the more than $67 billion the federal government spends on R&D each year, with the capability of leveraging this investment into commercial innovation, thus increasing the economic value of the entire package.

Small Business Innovation Research (SBIR) Grants

The only other federal partnership program that broadly supports commercial innovation is the Small Business Innovation Research (SBIR) grant (National Research Council 1999; State Science and

Technology Institute 1999). This is actually many programs run by each of the agencies purchasing R&D from the private sector under a mandate from the Congress and monitored by the Small Business Administration. This program arose from the congressional intent that federal agencies should be required to purchase a minimum fraction of their R&D procurement from small businesses. Initially focused on the Defense Department, where the R&D was intended to enhance government's ability to buy military goods and services, the program proved politically very attractive. It now covers all federal R&D agencies, and the minimum percentage has been expanded to 2.5 percent per year. Thus in the aggregate, SBIR, through which $9 billion flowed from Federal agencies to individual firms in the period 1983 to 1998 through 50,000 SBIR grants and contracts, dispenses substantially larger sums than does ATP, with approximately $1 billion expended in 1999 alone. Indeed, SBIR is the single largest source of competitive early stage research and technology development funding in the country for small businesses (State Science and Technology Institute 1999: 2). However, the size of the SBIR grants are specified by Congress, and they are typically smaller than those of ATP. The initial Phase I grant is up to $100,000 and supports research leading to a product concept. Success in this phase enables a firm to apply for a Phase II award of up to $750,000 for commercialization.[8] These two phases conceptually address the financial and research gaps that must be closed before a firm can expect significant levels of venture funding. Phase III, which does not entail any federal financial support, represents the commercialization of the technology using only private assets.

SBIR is enormously popular politically, as can be understood by its very wide geographic coverage, its relatively simple application and review procedures, and three administrative features of great political value: (a) no funds have to be specifically appropriated for SBIR grants; it is a tax levied on all the research agency budgets; (b) it is managed as an R&D program, fitting into the pattern of federal technology procurements developed during the cold war; and (c) the grants are constrained by law to be sufficiently small that it is unlikely that competitors who have not received SBIR grants will complain of market distortions. Unhappily, the ATP does not share any of these three features, although it should be noted that while conservatives often speculate that government support of one firm might disadvantage another, the ATP has apparently not experienced such complaints.

Venture Capitalists' Views of Federal Innovation Promotion

Venture capital executives are understandably skeptical of suggestions that government should participate in the same market they serve. They emphasize the importance they attach to hands-on management of new ventures, of the critical importance of moving quickly in dynamic markets, of the networks of personal relationships on which they depend so strongly in evaluating the risks they face. On the other hand, they also recognize that some other source of finance must be available to entrepreneurs to prepare their commercial ideas to the point where they are mature enough for the multi-million dollar investments the VC firms prefer to make. Thus David Morgenthaler states, "[I]t does seem that early stage help by the government in developing platform technologies and financing scientific discoveries is directed exactly at the areas where institutional venture capitalists cannot and will not go. In the analogy of the horse race, the role of government can be to improve the bloodlines of the horses and give them some preliminary schooling." (Morgenthaler 2000: 107–108).

Robert Charpie, chairman of Ampersand Ventures, observed that, from the point of view of a venture capitalist, "technical risk is the easiest" sort of risk to work with. "At the same time," he said,

It is natural for the government to focus on technical risk, because that's the sort of risk that is familiar to the government, which has extensive experience with large technical projects. There is no role from my point of view for government as an equity investor in start-ups. I don't want an investor who isn't interested in making money. It's hard enough to organize and create a successful business—to discipline a company, to drive people who are all anxious to be successful, to work hard, to make a lot of money. I can't tolerate the handicap of having an investor sitting at the table whose interest is in something else, like promoting the development of a technology in ways beyond the needs of the company.

The motives of private investors and government technology agencies are quite different, yet in the ATP model, for example, both are sharing costs and risks of high technology ventures. Josh Lerner explores the government programs, taking the view that these activities, even when focused on technology spillovers, can be viewed as an alternative form of venture investment. He notes that venture capitalists, in the aggregate, make a disproportionate contribution to innovation and growth. Venture capital has undergone a lot of change and growth, yet it is still just a fraction of a percent of public equity markets. The kinds of firms backed by venture capitalists often have a difficult time getting funded from more traditional financial sources, for reasons including uncertainty, information gaps and asymmetries, intangibility of assets, and shifts in market conditions.

Venture capitalists address particular problems associated with funding high-risk, early-stage technology firms using three sets of tools, which include sorting, governance, and certification/stamp of approval. (For more detail, see Josh Lerner, "When Bureaucrats Meet Entrepreneurs" in the NIST/ATP Report.) With regard to "public venture" programs, some of the questions/problems that arise are:

• Venture industry itself is highly focused in a few areas. Does it make sense for the government to target these areas, or should it perhaps look at other areas? How should government balance the competing social goals of achieving geographic diversity of development and achieving a high rate of return to the economy?

• How well suited are companies that are generally involved in contract research to the task of developing new commercial technologies?[9] Can or should a program like ATP avoid the contract research firms in favor of more entrepreneurial ones, or is it appropriate to favor those who make a business by developing technical knowledge?

• The ATP and other public programs are oriented to funding pre-commercial work; this orientation may not match up well with the rush to market typical in the entrepreneurial setting.

Lerner's view is that if ATP and SBIR are viewed as "public venture capitalist" programs, they will have all of the problems that conventional VCs have, and in addition, a number of problems that private VCs do not have:

• The government agency may not have access to proprietary information at the level of detail that would permit it to perform the appropriate level of due diligence before the "investment";

• An inappropriate "investment" tool (grant or contract instead of equity investment) mandated by Congress may not be optimally motivating;

• The degree of government oversight of the enterprise receiving the finds is limited by the traditional reluctance of government to micromanage its commercial contractors, a reluctance not shared by VC firms;

• The agencies are required to document their decisions, which might make agencies resist changes in plans, or cause firms to be reluctant to request such changes, even when the market would require it;

• There may be external distortions, such as pressures for regional distribution, or "gaming" behavior by repeat winners; since their goal is expressly to address market failures, agencies cannot completely duplicate the strategies of private industry, but instead must project and factor into their equation social returns on capital;

• If their mission precludes them from funding a company that can gain access to private sources of capital without government help, they may be driven to fund poorly managed firms or firms with structural problems.

Thus Lerner's examination of the consequences of measuring ATP success by the tests of the venture investor—successful market entry, equity value growth, and return on investment—serves to remind us that this is not a realistic model for a government program of this kind. Even if it were, a better strategy might be for government to share financial risks with private sources of equity investment, which are not constrained in the way government is.

Our conclusion is that ATP should be viewed as a *technological research* program, and not as a *public venture capital* program. The government would still attempt to measure success by the extent of successful commercialization of research, but also by evidence of successful technology diffusion. In this case business success is an important mechanism, but not a necessary condition for diffusion success. A project that was technically successful but failed in the market might be published and used by others in more promising markets. It might still fulfill the long term goal, set by the Congress, of creating useful technical knowledge that provides the nutrients for future economic growth. This is just the way ATP managers ask that their program be judged, but many conservatives continue to criticize it, even as they support SBIR.

Innovation: The Unnatural Act

This book deals with a highly improbable activity—creating new technologies that deliver new capabilities to society. We know from the skewness in the outcomes of such innovations (see Chapter IV and the paper contributed by Scherer and Harhoff) that, while the payoffs can be enormous, most often they are marginally acceptable or even disappointing. The skills required for successful innovation call for high levels of creativity, imagination, daring, technical knowledge, and business acumen. These are not the average capabilities in firms, universities, or government. There is nothing average about innovation. Yet, ask any business leader, politician, or economist, What should be the economic strategy of a democratic market economy like that of the United States? The reply will most likely be, "This is the age of information, the onset of a New Economy, in which science-based innovations can create the profits, the productivity growth and the prospect of some very big winners leading to whole new industries. Capital and labor productivity no longer define the limits to economic growth. The future belongs to the risk-taker, the entrepreneur." Indeed, the behavior of the NASDAQ equity market suggests that the Americans of modest circumstance, investing in their 401K retirement funds, believe it too.

But if this unnatural act of innovation is to become the mainstream strategy of the economy, we must think about how to build the institutional structures, the public policies, the skills and culture, in short how to create the social capital that might convert the unnatural act of innovation to something we all understand and know how to do. The United States cannot become an innovative society if the social capital to do it efficiently is restricted to the two coasts and a few other high-tech centers.

What is the challenge to the innovators? The reality we have tried to describe is admittedly somewhat chaotic. We observe that the most serious difficulty facing innovators is not the lack of a research strategy for realizing their inventions in practice; science-based ideas for new products and processes abound. Instead, the difficulties have their origin in gaps in the ability of inventors and the investor/managers to understand and trust one another; gaps in funding for the research not yet performed, without which investor/managers cannot feel justified in risking their client's money; institutional barriers to risk-taking that reflect poor fits between a firm's experience and the culture of innovation.

The "purely" technical risks are in some respects the easiest to deal with. None of the innovators, or the executives who invest in their ideas, told us they did not know how to go about performing the technological research required to define the product functions and costs and allow the innovation to proceed to product development, production, and marketing. This is because a sweeping change has come over the nature of technical risk-taking in the last half-century. Where the market is well understood, reducing technical risks (which amounts to understanding the design, materials, and processes well enough to allow commercialization) has itself become a science.

But that does not make the task easy. For even though the risks in radical innovations are not primarily technical, the barriers to their reduction lie outside the realm of science itself. Those barriers are still formidable. Venture capital managers are typically much more concerned about the difficulty of understanding market behavior and about finding managers who can bring focus to the task of innovation. Product managers in larger firms are often reluctant to champion innovations that lie outside the company's core business interests, unless the firm's business is innovation. Scientists and engineers, who believe in their own inventions, rarely lack confidence in their own ability to overcome the vagaries of nature and make their dream a commercial reality. But they worry that their bosses or investors do not understand the technology enough to share this confidence. All of these difficulties, however, come back to haunt the technical team, because the goal of risk reduction through research is constantly uncertain and shifting.

For unnatural acts of innovation to have high probabilities of success the participants need a simple environment in which the number of interacting institutions is small, where the necessary information on which trust and cooperation rest is equally available to all participants, and the innovation can take place without unduly changing the very environment on which it depends.

Unfortunately these simple conditions are becoming increasingly rare, for the innovation process is also becoming more complex. As we look to the future we see a global economy with high levels of technical skills in many nations. However atypical are the conditions for successful innovation, the incentives will increase competition, will force shorter product cycles, and will heighten the importance of fine-tuning product specifications to markets, all in the face of a set of available technical options that seem to grow exponentially.

What might this future look like? What might it require from all our institutions, public and private? We can only begin to explore that landscape.

Notes

1. They include technology spillovers (other firms benefit from the investing firm's R&D effort); market spillovers (new products stimulate creative dislocations in existing markets); and intellectual property rights (IPR) regimes that either reward innovating firms inadequately (undermining incentives to undertake innovative projects in the short term) or excessively (stifling innovation in subsequent product "generations").

2. This claim is supported by decades of empirical (Mansfield et al. 1977; Jones and Williams 1998) as well as theoretical (Nelson 1959; Arrow 1962; Shell 1966, 1973: 77–100) work on the divergence between private and public returns from innovation. It is important to note, however, that there is no overriding *a priori* theoretical reason to believe that, from a social standpoint, private firms will systematically underinvest in R&D. While imperfect appropriability arguments suggests that private incentives to innovate may be inadequate, other factors—in particular, the duplication of research effort aimed at the same or similar outcomes—may lead to overinvestment in R&D (see Spence 1984, Dasgupta and Maskin 1987).

3. Information provided by NIST-ATP, <www.atp.gov/www/99road/rslide10.htm>

4. The ATP statute originated in the Omnibus Trade and Competitiveness Act of 1988 (Public Law 100-418, 15 U.S.C. 278n), but was amended by the American

Technology Preeminence Act of 1991 (Public Law 102-245). The full text of the ATP statute is available at <http://www.atp.nist.gov/eao/ir-6099/statute.htm>.

5. For the many reports on ATP effectiveness assessment see <www.atp.nist.gov/eao/overview.htm>.

6. For additional information see the ATP publications web page, <http://www.atp.nist.gov/atp/pubs.htm>.

7. The contrast between the way ATP views failure and the way failure was addressed in Howard Frank's description of DARPA is striking. It emphasizes the fact that ATP is not a "pure" technology program but accepts the commitment to outcomes measured in economic as well as technical terms.

8. The actual objectives of phases I and II are worded somewhat vaguely: Phase I determines "the scientific and technical merit and feasibility of ideas" while Phase II is "to further develop the proposed ideas."

9. A frequently expressed policy concern about the SBIR program is the apparent success of "SBIR mills," firms whose business model seems to be competing for government R&D projects rather than focusing on commercialization.

Will Industry Fund the Science and Technology Base for the Twenty-First Century?

Mary L. Good

I spent four years in the Clinton Administration as the Under Secretary for Technology in the U.S. Department of Commerce (1993–97), where I was responsible for the oversight of the National Institute of Standards and Technology (NIST), which manages the Advanced Technology Program (ATP). The first two years of my tenure I was able to discuss the attributes of ATP and request significant funding levels for it. The program grew from about $60 million to over $200 million in that period. During the last two years, however, I spent a great deal of time explaining the program, discussing the assessments being done, and defending the management of the program. Beginning with the new Congress elected for the 1994 term, our objective was to maintain the program at its 1994 level and prevent, to the extent that we could, the politicization of the program. Today however, I can look back objectively on the program from the perspective of the private citizen who has an interest in the health of the innovation infrastructure of the country and who worries about our technology base for 2010 and beyond, when my grandchildren will be responsible for the prosperity and standard of living in the United States.

Thus, this paper reflects my observations and assumptions of the value of ATP, based on thirteen years as an industrial research manager in technology-intensive companies (Allied Signal and its predecessor companies); four years of intense involvement (and research) with the civilian technology base in the United States and abroad; and two years as an active member of a group of investors who seek to stimulate start-up and early-stage, technology-intensive companies in Arkansas and the mid-South, an area that has a very poor track record for these activities. Thus my remarks present an opinion based on close study in several arenas: the art of technology development in an industry dependent on technology for profits and growth; technology development stimulated by government programs; and technology development that leads to a venture-fundable business start-up.

I participated in ATP as a grantee, managing an ATP project on metallic glasses for Allied Signal, before I came to the government. My vision of the program then was to leverage ATP support to increase my chances of getting internal company support for a technology program I thought had significant long-term commercial potential for our company. Our ATP grant allowed us to contract with some experts in the field at two different universities and to develop a prototype for a commercial process to make metallic glasses. The grant fit all of the rhetorical conditions we have come to associate with ATP: early technology development, enabling technology, collaborative work with university research groups, and the creation of a truly new material. The program was a success from the company's point of view, although we did not accomplish all of the technical goals we had originally set. The company has commercialized the process and now sells significant products in a financially successful business. Since the technology was not considered as part of our core business at the time, the ATP grant made it possible to pursue what became a successful product line. It was government support for a large company whose expensive equipment and experienced technologists that made the development possible. In my view, it would have been beyond the resource limits and capability of most small firms.

I have also reviewed all of the many studies of ATP outcomes. Clearly the program has produced winners in a number of cases, from enabling technology licensed to a wide variety of users, to the establishment of companies marketing truly new products. In fact, the number of failures is perhaps lower than one might like to see because it indicates that the level of risk-taking may be sub-optimal. For example, the success rate is better than that experienced by venture-funded start-ups and early-stage technology companies.

However, I believe that most objective observers would agree that ATP has been a successful program in supporting technology research that provides a pathway to commercial innovation. Thus in my mind the question is not whether the program works, but why it is needed.

The most frequent argument used against ATP is that the private sector should provide the resources to do any and all research beyond fundamental university research, either using current company resources or by the acquisition of capital support from such sources as venture capital firms and angel investors. Our attention then should be on studies that can determine the probability that the nation's innovation system is being adequately addressed by the private sector. An historical study would suggest that early governmental support has been a factor in many of our major innovations; the telegraph and aviation are early and dramatic examples. The many studies already done on the origins of our current exploitation of information technology clearly point out the government role, particularly that of DARPA, in its funding of early technology research to develop the underlying technologies for the Internet and computer systems. The technologies that made the agricultural revolution possible in the United States were almost all developed through technology research programs in the Department of Agriculture.

True, there have been catastrophic failures in government programs. The one most cited (and, I might add, most used to argue against ATP) is the Department of Energy syn-fuel program in the mid-1970s. Knowing something about that program, I would suggest that its biggest failure was to allow the politics of the day to dictate costly "quick fix" demonstration projects, rather than focusing on the technology research that needed to be done prior to the design of large, complex pilot plants.

In any case, a good analysis of government support for technology research in this century would show a return on investment probably equal or superior to that enjoyed by our innovative companies in the same period. In addition, that support has largely been at the early stage of a technology, where the private sector is least likely to provide the seed money to get it from a promising idea to recognizable commercial potential. The real success of our system has been the ability of our established companies and our entrepreneur and venture-capital communities to discern quickly where commercial opportunities may arise from early-technology research, and to make the investment necessary to assess the market fully and do the innovation necessary to bring the technology to a successful commercial outcome. Thus, ATP and sister programs should be judged on where they fit in to the innovation system of the nation, including an evaluation of the country's complex portfolio of research and development in the private sector, the not-for-profit sector, and the government.

The Council on Competitiveness has recently done such an analysis (Council on Competitiveness, 1999); a close read of its report on innovation would provide feelings of comfort about our current development of commercial products but also feelings of concern about whether our investment in next-generation technology is adequate to provide the United States with the opportunity to be a leader in the next global business cycle. The investments by the National Institutes of Heath (NIH) and the pharmaceutical industry have clearly given us a commanding lead in biotechnology in almost all of its aspects. This lead can be expected to persist for quite some time, both because of the magnitude of our lead and because NIH continues to fund basic science that is close to the potential technology. Moreover (although this is not a highly publicized fact), NIH funds early-technology development that moves quickly into commercialization processes of the pharma-firms. Today U.S. research in the life sciences is roughly $26–28 billion annually, with NIH funding about half of that. Of all the models that indicate the values of government research, both fundamental and applied, the successes of the biotechnology and pharmaceutical industries are stellar examples.

However, the Council finds that in other technology-based commercial areas, the commitment to research is much weaker both in the industry and in the government. Research and development in information technology is dominated by the development of new applications for technology that is already beyond the true research stage. Indeed, most of the venture capital money in Silicon Valley now goes to new companies with innovative ideas for exploiting today's technologies. Both David Morgenthaler of Morgenthaler

Ventures and Richard Burnes of Charles River Ventures made comments to that effect at the MTR practitioner's workshop in June 1999. Mr. Morgenthaler made the point that venture capitalists do not develop enabling technologies, and that their fortes are in the use of enabling technologies to develop a product, the revision and improvement of a product, or the creative metamorphosis of a product into an application in a new arena. Mr. Burnes made the point that in the 1970s and 1980s, venture capitalists did see "technically sophisticated projects, where there was a lot of technical risk, and they took that risk." However, he followed that comment with the observation that venture capital activities are now in a phase "where there are many, many opportunities that the existing technologies can address and create major companies."

The question then becomes: who is financing the early-technology research that will lead to new technologies? Apart from James McGroddy of IBM, the panel of business executives at the June MTR workshop did not create the impression that the industries they represent would support the early-technology research necessary to develop a proof of principle or a "bread-board" prototype. They talked about "process systems" that let one assess risk before an investment is made, about how to determine if potential products would fit in their companies' business plans, and about the need to determine whether the project will have a potential market of a size to be of interest to a large company (maybe $50 million is the cut-off). None of these comments gives you the feeling that these will be the avenues for truly new technology development. One very promising theme of their remarks, however, was the realization that innovation is a "people" activity and that the involvement of really good people, both technical and managerial, is the key to the successful commercial exploitation of research of any kind.

The remarks of the business executives are very much in line with the results of on-going analysis of current industry R&D trends by the Industrial Research Institute, the National Science Foundation, and others. All of these studies indicate that the percentage of industrial R&D devoted to basic or applied research is small compared to the resources expended for product and process improvement and technical services. In industries where new products move rapidly into the market, such as personal computers, companies rarely have significant technology investments beyond the next model to be released. In the current global environment where quality, price, and time-to-market are the differentiating business parameters, this use of technical talent and capital resources is neither unexpected nor necessarily bad. It just means that the fundamental technology pool available for true innovations is not being replenished by these firms.

A very good overview of the innovation in industry was presented in the *Economist* magazine of February 20, 1999. Several specific assessments in that article are relevant to the present discussion:

• One-third of all of the world's venture capital today goes to nurturing innovation in Silicon Valley. Most of the money is raised there, most of the entrepreneurs have moved there, and most of the wealth created stays there.

• The *Economist* argues that the most likely rival to Silicon Valley is Israel with its immigrant technical workforce, competitive environment, respect for learning, and willingness to take risks. It reports that Israel has 135 engineers and technicians per 10,000 people, compared to only 18 in the United States.

• The typical strategy for venture-funded businesses has changed over the last year or two: going public is less common, as more firms are being bought out by established companies seeking to shore up their innovation product streams.

• The international competition in innovation is heating up. Of the world's top 300 international companies, those headquartered in Denmark, Sweden, Canada, and the United States have increased their industrial R&D spending by 17–26 % from 1996 to 1997. During the same period, similar firms in Britain and Italy increased their average R&D spending by only 3–5%. In Finland, notably, comparable companies spend an average of over 10% of sales on R&D, while U.S. firms in the same cohort spend about 5% of sales. (Perhaps the success of Finland's Nokia cellular telephone company is no fluke.)

• The *Economist* article argues that "innovation has more to do with the pragmatic search for opportunity than with romantic ideas about serendipity or lonely pioneers pursuing their vision against all odds." It states that the new industrial cycle fueled by information technology has probably run through two-thirds of its life-cycle, leaving only a 5–10 year window before some new wave of technology begins.

• The Stevenson-Wydler Technology Innovation Act and the Bayh-Dole Act have had a significant impact on American innovation, says the *Economist*, because they have fostered government-industry-university interactions, which have speeded up the exploitation of not-for-profit research, allowed private companies to partner with government, and let university researchers "cash in" on their government-funded expertise.

These reports, reviews, and economic studies, along with personal observations, lead me to believe that the current industrial structure will not provide the same level of technology pool for the country's innovators to draw from in the future as has been provided in the past fifty years. That technology pool was a mix of heavily funded corporate laboratories that created more technology than they used in-house, and government funding of fundamental research and early technology research, especially at DARPA and NASA. On the government side, the current climate is not conducive to replacing DARPA and NASA in their role in technology research, and the defense budget continues to de-emphasize this type of activity.

On the industry side, there are some significant bright spots where industry is carrying out research on truly new technologies. Two that come to mind immediately are Xerox PARC and Lucent's Bell Laboratories. A review of Xerox's web page indicates the breadth of its "out-in-front" new technology research, ranging from next-generation technology for document handling to truly new technology like MEMS (Micro-Electro-Mechanical-Systems), "smart matter," and nanotechnology. Bell Labs' new venture has created new business structures to capture promising new technologies discovered by Bell Labs researchers. Other similar industrial laboratories have also done significant work in the development of truly new technologies. However, they are not likely to create spin-offs like those that resulted from the technologies that escaped from Xerox PARC in the 1970s or that created Intel from

Shockley's transistor, first conceived at Bell Labs. The new generations of research managers and business executives at these companies have worked hard to shape the forefront research so that they can capture most of the value. Thus the pool of new start-ups in new technologies outside of the biotech area will come primarily from the academic laboratories, the government laboratories, and the government-sponsored partnerships like ATP, and perhaps from continuing programs from NASA and the Defense Department.

There are many justifications for programs like ATP, and most of them have been well articulated in the past few years. Two really important reasons that have not received attention from ATP or the policy community, however, are the needs to provide opportunity to entrepreneurs in all parts of the country, and the need to support subject areas not currently considered fashionable by the usual providers of capital. Good ideas do not arise only in Silicon Valley and Austin, Texas. They occur all over the country and, if properly nourished, they could be the seedlings of new centers of innovation activity. The same is true for innovative ideas in areas other than information technology and biotechnology, which absorb most of the current venture capital resources. The concept of nurturing new technology to the point where its potential commercial value can be determined should be a priority of the national innovation policy. It should be supported through incentives to state governments, programs like SBIR (Small Business Innovation Research) and ATP, and incentives for investors to place at least some of their risk capital in early-stage technology research which has high risk but also high potential to become a "change agent" product or process.

ATP has been studied more than any comparable program ever! It has been shown to deliver results from a well-conceived and well-run rigorous review process that is not subject to political bias. However, it has been plagued by ideological debates, identification as a "Clinton" program, and year-to-year funding that resembles the "perils of Pauline." I would hope that in the next year or two, it can be stabilized with funding in the $500 million per year range, and that it could be focused on technologies that are not fundable (or at least not funded) in other agencies and are not in vogue in the private capital community. The projects could be selected very much as they are now and the mix of large companies, start-ups, or early-stage companies and consortia could be controlled to be sure adequate attention is given to small and embryonic companies with good ideas. Larger companies should not be eliminated, however, because they can bring a range of opportunities which they would not pursue on their own but where they have resources and expertise to bring projects to a satisfactory conclusion with some wins and some losses.

If appropriate research and policy strategy could position ATP as a strategic piece of the government's research portfolio, to provide opportunity for entrepreneurs in any location and in areas of corporate and government neglect, I believe bipartisan political support could be achieved. The quality of the peer review, the vision of new technology development, and the business incentive process could all still be maintained. This would clearly circumvent any political attempt to reposition the program to fund politically popular research areas or to rework the management and selection criteria each year. This rationale could also be used to appeal to the states to provide matching funds, create incentives for local investors, and get congressional delegations on board.

I am an advocate of a balanced federal R&D portfolio that includes: first, fundamental research that is not targeted to any foreseeable commercial use; second, applied research designed to provide answers to specific scientific and technical questions, and needed to carry out certain government missions in defense, energy, space, the environment, and underlying national interests in the commercial sector such as standards and meteorology; and third, technology research that provides incentives for the development of new technologies before the usual market forces will focus on them, and that will provide significant additions to the country's technology pool. A portfolio of this mix will provide universities with funding for knowledge creation research, an opportunity to partner with industry in applied areas, and support for the education and training of the next generation of our technical workforce. It allows mission agencies to meet the new demands on their knowledge base, and it creates new technologies that create new businesses. The portfolio also provides private-sector investors with a variety of opportunities to create growth for both new and existing businesses.

What I am truly advocating is a research policy for federal investments that will serve as well during the next fifty years as federally-funded health and national security R&D have served us over the past fifty years. After about fifty years of experience in investing in research and people in a rather opportunistic way, it is time the public had an innovation investment policy that is as good as that practiced by the forefront companies who will be players in the next technology wave, whatever it turns out to be.

The Changing Landscape: Innovators, Firms, and Government

In the twentieth century ... the individual inventor is becoming rare; men with the power of originating are largely absorbed into research institutions of one kind or another, where they must have expensive equipment for their work. Useful invention is to an ever-increasing degree issuing from the research laboratories of large firms which alone can afford to operate on an appropriate scale.... Invention has become more automatic, less the result of intuition or genius and more a matter of deliberate design.
—John Jewes, David Sawers, and Richard Stillerman, *The Sources of Invention* (1959), quoted in Rhodes (1999:12)

Invention is a fundamental component of the human experience. Science, as a method of discovery, is a particular "invention" whose entire history occupies only the most recent sliver of the human chronology. Yet the power of science is such that it has all but subsumed invention. Where invention had for millennia signified brilliant moments of individual inspiration, in the past fifty years it has become much more of a process, a methodical search perhaps leading to discovery—a process itself subject to systematic understanding and mastery. While still critically dependent on creativity, insight, even genius, invention has become scientific.[1]

Science-based *innovation*—at least in the sense of the term employed by scholars and by the authors of this book—is also a recent phenomenon.[2] Before the advent of science and large-scale markets, the boundary between a technical breakthrough and a marketable product scarcely existed. As a rule, the breakthrough was the product. Only in the past century have the two become distinct.

How did this happen? Both technological and institutional factors were critical. The mid-twentieth century was a watershed for science. While atomic, molecular, and nuclear sciences were born in the 1920s and 1930s, it was largely in the United States during World War II (with the nation's research apparatus under an unprecedented degree of federal control) that science changed from an activity largely based on experiment and description to one founded on empirically validated theoretical models. The development of a vast array of new research tools led to an equally staggering acquisition of quantitative, empirical knowledge. This knowledge, in turn, permitted the generation of the theoretical models from which the properties of nature could be not only understood but accurately predicted. In this sense, science itself became "scientific."[3]

As science became scientific, so did engineering. Working from the growing body of reliable theory, engineers were now able to design materials to fit specific needs, rather than relying upon the materials provided by nature. (Today, designer molecules, genetically modified organisms, synthetic materials, and the now-emerging nano-technologies all greatly expand the potential scope for innovation.) In particular, engineers seeking to turn a good idea into a prototype—a marketable product of predictable and acceptable specifications—were increasingly able to rely upon new science, rather than being forced to create prototypes by trial and error.

Changes in science and engineering were paralleled by changes in institutional forms. While today's large research university descends directly from the classically focused universities of the last century, it bears as little actual resemblance to its ancestors as today's venture capital firm does to the merchant banks of the 1900s. Today's research universities are still judged above all on their effectiveness in educating students and expanding the frontiers of knowledge, but they are increasingly expected to generate the ideas—if not the prototypes—for tomorrow's new goods and services. "What is the source of innovation?" MIT President Charles Vest (2000: 323) asks rhetorically. "Our universities must be an important part of the chain of innovation, both in the creation of new knowledge and ideas and in the education of people."[4]

Similarly, the marketplace advantage of the large technology-based corporation depends increasingly on the ability to routinely convert inventions into successful products, and decreasingly on raw economies of scale and scope. As noted by Vest (2000: 322): "Industry today, as we say over and over, is increasingly knowledge-based. It is global, driven by innovation. It is digitally connected and created by entrepreneurs."

Yet while recognizing the powerful incentives that exist toward making invention and innovation, in the aggregate, become all but routine, we must keep clearly in mind that, at the level of the particular project, success at science-based innovation is anything but routine. Indeed, the environments that foster technological innovation—institutions, networks of relationships, culture and traditions—are as exceptional as successful innovations themselves. Such social capital, often geographically localized, both supports invention and provides an infrastructure to guide inventions to the marketplace with a reasonable chance of commercial success.[5] Helping to create and support such social capital is among the most important and difficult challenges for public policy in the coming century.

Long-Term Trends Driving Change in the U.S. Innovation System

The Blending of Market and Technical Uncertainties

In this volume we have found that separating the task of reducing technical risks from the problem of market definition is difficult, if not impossible; in the future the two will be increasingly blended. Those concerned primarily about the ultimate market viability of an innovation will want to influence the technology earlier in the cycle. If the prototype products are to be market-tested even before the technology is in place to permit high-volume production, more early funding will be needed to establish a robust pilot line. The pressure to achieve early market entry will be doubly difficult in the face of the need to shorten product cycles.

The Internet suggests an interesting pattern that might emerge. Perhaps the main reason "dot.com" business has had such an extraordinary growth is because of a deliberately designed feature of Internet architecture: There are virtually no inherent structural barriers to access to the distribution system that the Internet and the world wide web provide, which allows software innovators to introduce their products to the market when they are still in prototype stage. Sometimes the product release is referred to as an "alpha test" of the product and its market, a phrase intended to warn the user that the product is still immature. Often the offering might better be called "test-marketing." But in this process both the innovator and the customers are engaged in a cooperative activity of concurrent technical and market development. One could not easily say which risk is being reduced first: technical or market.

It will not be as easy to adopt this strategy in other industries, where there are structural barriers to this kind of producer-user collaboration. The pharmaceutical industry, for example, cannot be allowed to test its new drugs on the open market until government has assured the public of their efficacy and safety. But even in this case, government allows qualified physicians to use experimental drugs in approved research programs, especially when the patients are seriously ill and have few alternatives.

The Increasing Number of Participants in the Innovation System

Even where the dot.com model of concurrent development and marketing is possible, it implies a widening circle of individuals who must share knowledge and pursue their differing goals in a trusting, collaborative manner. The circle must include not only the inventor, the business manager, and the VC but also other institutions, whose contributions to the innovation are called "complementary assets" (Teece 1987). A computer system to increase the flow of traffic on busy highways will depend not only on an information technology producer, the municipality to which he might sell it, and the investors prepared to finance it, but also on the producers of the application software, the U.S. Department of Transportation's safety standards, and the automobile manufacturers who will have to sell and install the end-user equipment.

None of these other actors is standing still. When the innovation is introduced, they will react either to foster the innovation's chances or perhaps to frustrate them. The economy responds dynamically to the introduction of radical innovations.

A model of the technology development process proposed by Henry Ergas has the virtue of recognizing the dynamic nature of science-based innovations, which change the environments within which they are launched and thus alter the nature of the risks encountered (Ergas 1989, quoted in Branscomb and Choi 1996: 202–208). This model comprises four stages: *generation* (all the R&D up to initial production); *application* (the commercialization phase, including manufacturing and initial customer acceptance); *verticalization* (changes induced in the behavior or technology of suppliers, customers, and end-users), and *diffusion* (regulatory, environmental, even cultural changes brought about by the innovation). All four stages must run their course before the magnitude of returns and future prospects for growth can be ascertained. The social capital to facilitate that growth must embrace many more participants than the producer and its customers. Small wonder that technical risk alone cannot predict the observed magnitude of skew in investment returns from such innovations. Those concerned primarily about the ultimate market viability of the innovation will want to influence the technology earlier in the cycle. If the prototype products are to be market tested even before the technology is in place to permit high-volume production, more early funding will be needed to establish a robust pilot line. The pressure to achieve early market entry will be doubly difficult in the face of the need to shorten product cycles.

Growing Technological Complexity in the Innovation System

As product cycles have become increasingly compressed, technologies themselves have become increasingly complex. The next generation of innovative breakthroughs will require levels of interdisciplinary cooperation and coordination previously unknown in modern science. Speaking from the perspective of the academic researcher, Vest (2000: 321) states: "We have a responsibility, whether we are life scientists, engineers, physicists, or mathematicians, to keep people aware of the way in which our different disciplines interact. The race to sequence the genome is an example. That, of course, involves biology, by definition. But, in fact, the clever use of combinatorial mathematics, robotics, engineering, and automation is making the whole venture possible."

Drivers of Continued Growth in Science-based Innovation

In such an environment, is it possible to begin to anticipate the future path of technical progress—not to mention the even more complex path of market acceptance of new technologies? As Steve Kent of BBN notes (and as the skewness of economic returns demonstrates), even if the underlying technology is stable, it is difficult to predict the particular form of a product or service that will come to dominate the market. It may well come from an industry with quite a different business model, a different set of interfaces to other industries, and a different way of delivering value to customers.[6]

Jim McGroddy points out that one can, to some extent, project technical trends into the future by tracing out the trajectory of progress for underlying technologies—an example is Moore's Law for processing speed in computer chips. In McGroddy's view, relatively stable, predictable long-term trends in technological progress underlie punctuated eras of expanded market opportunities:

All the great waves of technology that we've seen [have the property] that while there's usually exponential progress in some parametric characterization of the goodness of the technology, that continuous exponential improvement in the technology causes discontinuous things to happen high in the value chain. At a certain point, the horsepower per weight is enough that you can make this thing called a flying machine. And it opens this huge amount of opportunity.... There's a huge amount of work that's driving forward this exponential progress. In the case of integrated circuit technology ... there's at least two orders of magnitude to go in the next ten years.... So it's a perfectly reasonable behavior on the part of society to focus on the applications of stuff.

The explanation for this continuous progress in technological performance is, of course, a sequence of radical changes in the science underlying the technology, each following a period of evolutionary improvement. When one technology reaches the end of its extensibility and must be replaced by another, the new means for sustaining progress often emerge from a different industry, and may be the source of eras of new opportunity.

The boom in Internet start-ups over the past few years—the vast majority of which are testing the frontiers of business models, not technology—is evidence of the phenomenon described by McGroddy. Underlying the "IT revolution" has been the steady (and dramatic) growth in the power of information processing and storage capabilities. In contrast, the evolution of market opportunities—depending not only on technology, but also on behavior, beliefs, and infrastructure—has been much more discontinuous.

What is the next area of radical technical progress underlying dramatic changes in markets? The clear candidate is the impact of the biotechnology revolution on medical and agricultural products and services. This broad area of technology and market opportunity currently dominates university research output—for example, accounting for better than 75 percent of all citations of papers generated by the University of California system from 1988 to 1997 (Branstetter 2000).[7] The success of the Human Genome project (a fascinating story of public/private research in its own right) signals the beginning of a revolution in genomics about whose ultimate economic and social implications we can only begin to guess.

Further adding to a sense of optimism about the technological possibilities of the future are the dramatic upsurges in venture capital financing of new firms and in patenting activity in the second half of the 1990s. Do these portend a sustained era of broadly based technological progress? Or do they suggest that the "low-hanging fruit" have been picked, and remaining challenges will be more difficult? Experience over a few hundred years suggests that one should treat predictions of diminishing technological opportunities with skepticism. Addressing this precise issue more than a half century ago, Schumpeter (1942: 117–118) wrote:

We are just now in the downgrade of a wave of enterprise that created the electrical power plant, the electrical industry, the electrified farm and home and the motorcar. We find all that very marvelous, and we cannot for our lives see where opportunities of comparable importance are to come from. As a matter of fact, however, the promise held out by the chemical industry alone is much greater than what it was possible to anticipate in, say, 1880, not to mention the fact that the mere utilization of the achievement of the age of electricity and the production of modern homes for the masses would suffice to provide investment opportunities for quite a time to come.

In hindsight, we find apparent the wisdom of not betting against the human will to invent and innovate. Yet Schumpeter's insight was far less evident coming in the wake of a global economic depression and in the midst of a world war.[8]

A study by Kortum and Lerner (1999) provides us with some further guidance regarding our contemporary circumstances. It finds that the venture capital mode of financing is indeed particularly efficient in generating innovative output; this suggests that increases in venture funding portend higher levels of innovative productivity. In contrast, however, an examination of the sectoral distribution of venture financing during the 1990s reveals that over 60 percent of both the level and the growth of venture funding during this period went to Internet-related industries—a sector where, as we have noted, new ventures have not tended to be on the technological frontier.

The data on patents provide further information on long-term technological trends. Kortum and Lerner (1999) ask whether the observed surges during the 1990s in both patent applications and patents granted are best explained by changes in the propensity to patent (driven by changes in the legal environment); success by entrenched incumbents in influencing regulators in their favor; increasing technological opportunities in particular sectors (such as biotech and IT); or improved management of R&D (in particular, a shift toward more applied activities). Somewhat surprisingly—though less so in the context of the themes of this volume—the authors find that the evidence fails to support all of these hypotheses but the one pertaining to management of R&D: "By a process of elimination, our analysis leads us to conclude that the increase in patenting has been driven by changes in the management of innovation, involving a shift to more applied activities" (Kortum and Lerner 1999: 21). All of this means that the invention-innovation gaps must start to close. Yet we began this chapter noting that they have in fact been growing. To see how

Number of Patents

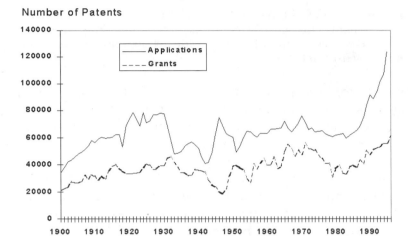

Figure VI-1 Patenting by U.S. inventors. Source: Kortum and Lerner (1999), figure 1.

these gaps might be closed we need to look again at the institutions that support the system of innovation.

Institutional Requirements for an Effective System of Innovation

In earlier chapters we have identified the institutional environment required for successful innovation. Among the requirements are these:

• A research environment that fosters creativity in basic science and engineering while encouraging the exploration of possible applications of social and economic value. Here the state and federal role in support of research universities and laboratories is essential.

• An institutional home for technical teams motivated and qualified to transform innovative ideas into practical economic opportunities, pursuing a research strategy with sufficient options to deal with unexpected technical problems. This strategy may require access to consultants, arrangements for collaboration with others facing similar challenges, and pursuit of more than one path to success. This home might be a university willing to pursue a commercial idea far enough to define the technology required, or might be an incubator or other form of nascent business entity.

• A business environment that supports innovations rather than seeing them as a threat to existing products, technologies, and revenue streams, as incompatible with existing business models, or as unqualified under technology-specific government regulations.

• A financial and entrepreneurial environment, including institutional sources of seed financing, managerial assistance, and early and accurate reporting of information from target markets, that encourages the creation of new firms for the exploitation of radical innovations.

• A network of institutions and relationships of trust that, taken together, constitute the support for successful systems of innovation, such as those in Silicon Valley, Route 128 Boston, and the North Carolina Research Triangle.

Serious deficiencies in any of the above institutional resources may constitute a non-pecuniary barrier to innovation. When all are present, the speed and efficiency with which the resources required for successful innovation can be brought to bear generates a very impressive competitive advantage. The key point is that business risks—technical, financial, marketing, and managerial—are shared by all the institutions in the network—banks, unions, schools, laboratories, services, transport, and communications. The trust underlying the collective sharing of both risks and rewards constitutes the essence of the social capital that is essential to an innovative economy (Branscomb 1996; Fountain 1998: 85–111).

The Sectoral and Geographic Concentration of Innovative Effort

Evidence of deficiency in institutional support for innovation can be seen quite clearly in the geographic concentration of innovation-based economic growth in the United States, primarily on the two coasts, and in the concentration of venture, debt, and equity investment capital in a very small number of economic sectors at any one time. For much of the past few years, the dot.com phenomenon distracted many investors. Figure VI-2 contrasts the distribution of VC investments among different industries in 1998 with

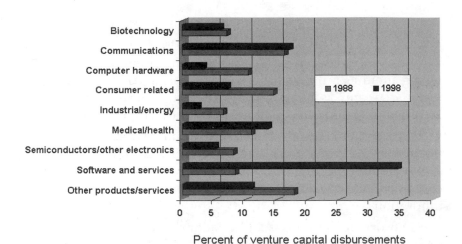

Percent of venture capital disbursements

Figure VI-2 U.S. venture capital disbursements, by industry category, 1988 and 1998. Source: U.S. National Science Board (2000), figure 7-25.

those of 1988. The concentration in software firms in 1998 was such that some VC executives even went so far as to claim, in the 1998 workshop, that they would not be looking at biotech at all in 1999. In the environment of the time they felt that they could recover their investment out of the dot.coms in five to six months, while it could take up to five years to get their money out of a biotech firm. The great variation from year to year in the sectors in which VC firms invest suggests a degree of "faddism" in this industry. One VC executive responded to the criticism that they "only look for pennies under the street light" with the reply that the VC business is dominated by the need to make their investors' assets liquid, which depends on the investment bankers on Wall Street who arrange for mergers and public stock offerings. If Wall Street pursues fads, so will the VC industry, the argument goes. It may be, of course, that focusing investment in certain emerging technologies takes advantage of shared information and reduced transaction costs, and this could be an efficient economic course.

Geographical concentration of innovative effort is at least as severe as sectoral concentration. As the Rust Belt gave way to the high-tech sector, the geographic concentration of successful research-based innovation shifted, too. The uneven distribution of innovation mirrors the equally uneven distribution of R&D in the United States. The top ten states perform two-thirds of all R&D in the nation; the top six—California, Michigan, New York, New Jersey, Massachusetts, and Texas—perform half. But the direction of cause and effect is not clear; robust R&D activity does not ensure a high level of innovation and its maturing into a significant economic asset. It seems more likely that these regions have the institutional and managerial assets, as well as the technical resources—in short, the social capital—to make productive use of R&D, and thus attract more of it.[9] Thus, a study of the economic returns from federal R&D expenditures in Massachusetts (Candell and Jaffe 1999: 510–530) showed that the level of federal R&D was positively correlated with economic growth in the state, suggesting that the conditions were favorable for converting that R&D into innovations.

Universities in Ohio, for example, have excellent research, but Silicon Valley dominates in the realm of financial rewards beyond the university. A study by Fogarty and Sinha (1999) compared Cleveland with Palo Alto and found that VCs evaluated the average small high-tech start-up in California at $12 million, while a similar enterprise in Cleveland was valued locally at just $4 million. One reason for such a discrepancy is the higher probability of value in Silicon Valley, given the strength of the talent pool and infrastructure there. A bidding war among VCs in Silicon Valley might also be helping to drive up valuations. This phenomenon may leave government R&D programs with an appropriate space to compensate for this sectoral concentration of private investment, in the interest of keeping many doors to economic growth open.

The degree of concentration of entrepreneurial activity in favored regions and in favored technologies may well be explained by the need for concentrations of key assets—research universities, an imaginative banking sector, highly efficient communications, and talented and flexible labor are often cited as important. Historically, like industries have tended to cluster—for example, machine tools in Dayton, Ohio, and textiles and banking in Charlotte, North Carolina. One might have expected that firms in the same industry would seek to avoid proximity with their competitors, but apparently the value of a shared infrastructure serving the industry's needs is more important. Investment risk clearly depends in part on the attributes of the economic environment that affect the likelihood that research-based innovations can take root and flourish.

Institutional Roles for Government

Where institutional and behavioral barriers impede the development of technologies with potentially broad economic benefits, government has a role as a steward for national economic policy and as a stimulator of advanced technical research. Democratic governments traditionally respond to apparent inequitable distributions of economic advantage. Thus, from the points of view of developing the national economy and of helping regions of the nation to take advantage of their research and entrepreneurial assets and ambitions, both state and federal governments have explored a number of possible roles. The primary focus of government investment has been in research, primarily through public and not-for-profit institutions. But in the quest for more effective coupling of research outputs with economic outcomes, both federal and state governments have experimented with private sector research partnerships.

The Advanced Technology Program (ATP)—the sponsor of the report that provided the basis for this volume—is a notable example of such partnerships. The ATP was established by Congress to help the private sector minimize one significant source of risk in science-based innovation: the transition from an attractive new product concept, based on new science, to a workable technology that enables product development and market entry. The research needed at this stage typically lies beyond the scope of the science involved, but short of the target for venture capital investment. The ATP has clearly demonstrated its ability to help firms bridge this "research gap" and thus enable a higher rate of innovation in areas most likely to bring broad economic benefits to the nation.[10] The participants in our workshops confirmed the existence of impediments to taking risks that can and should be lessened through both government and private action.

More generally, nations that once relied on science and technology policy, by which they usually meant public investments in scientific research, have come to realize that this supply-side policy would probably be ineffective without demand-side policies to put those ideas to work.[11] Thus there is now widespread acceptance of the idea that "science and technology policy" should be replaced by "research and innovation policy" (Branscomb and Keller 1998). The goals of an innovation policy are clear enough, even if the means for their attainment are not: full employment, decreased income disparities, rising real incomes, safe, healthy working conditions, and satisfying work. What policy tools, other than investing in research, can one use to encourage innovation? The list is long: economic policy, trade policy, tax policy and accounting rules, competition policy, regulation of equity markets and industry structure, intellectual property law, industrial relations, education and training, and the full range of environmental, health, and safety regulations.

This long list of policy tools would seem to offer a lot of options. In fact, these policies must also be seen as a set of potential barriers to innovation, set up one behind the other. Any one of them, if sufficiently mismanaged, can seriously discourage would-be innovators. It might seem obvious that all these economic issues should be dealt with by economic policy people who should recognize the value and the fragility of an economy increasingly based on science-based innovation. But since science policy mavens have for so long insisted (erroneously) that innovations happen automatically as a result of research, the economists have mostly left these issues to "science policy." And science policy does not enjoy a priority on political agendas anywhere near that of economic, trade, tax, or regulatory policy.

Furthermore, only a few of these policy tools (anti-trust law and intellectual property law are examples) can be used to create a positive, specific incentive to innovation; most of them exist for other reasons and must be examined to ensure that suppression of innovation is not an unwanted side effect. To ensure that every government agency is alert to this responsibility, a policy body at or near the top of government should be charged with monitoring agency diligence (Hart 1998). The challenge to governments is formidable because, as discussed earlier, building an innovative society requires developing the social capital of society, a task that most governments perform poorly even if they devote a lot of time and attention to it.

What, then, might be a more specific set of suggestions for public policy?

• Federal funding of university research must grow at a rate sufficient to support commercial R&D, which in the last decade grew twice as fast as academic science. As Mary Good points out, basic research funding cannot be expected to come from private sources, yet the innovation system is totally dependent on an expanding knowledge foundation.[12]

• At the same time, the federal government should balance its important investments in basic science with a strong program of basic technological research, an important component of which should be carried out in collaboration with technically competent, innovative firms, as provided for in the NIST ATP program.

• Government research support should do more to bridge the Valley of Death, by permitting the research universities to carry their technical ideas of commercial promise closer to the point where private investment will permit commercialization.

• To help create the social capital on which high-tech innovation depends, the federal agencies should look to the states for collaboration, should encourage the networking of firms, universities, federal laboratories, state innovation programs, VC and other investment firms, and a variety of other private and public institutions.

• To address current regional and sectoral imbalances in the propensity for innovation, the federal government should collaborate with states that have sound programs of investment, as was the case with North Carolina in the Research Triangle.

• The central institutions for making economic policy should give specific attention to those elements of economic policy that affect the incentives and the uncertainties associated with high-tech innovation.

Where should the federal government look for help and guidance on how to do this successfully? It should look to the states, many of which have deep experience with the mixture of technical and other assets required to build economic wealth; to universities, increasingly the source of inventions and entrepreneurial capacity; and to VC firms, whose network experience, pragmatism, financial acumen, and understanding of the human and organizational performance dimension of entrepreneurship, qualify them to advise government on how it can play a more constructive role in the early stage of the conversion from invention to innovation.

Future Directions for Innovation Policy

The market sets the bar that the innovator's research must clear. What might appear at first as a laboratory problem becomes enmeshed in the full complexity of all stages of the innovation process. Even if the innovation gains the confidence of investors and reaches the market successfully, there remain the greater risks of not enjoying a return over time that compensates for the inherent uncertainties of market acceptance and growth.

These uncertainties are exacerbated by gaps: institutional, financial, and sociological—perhaps even public policy—gaps that, taken together, define shortcomings in the social and public capital for innovation. The fact that favorable conditions for this kind of innovation seem confined to a few geographical areas and to a limited set of technologies and industries further emphasizes the fragility of the conditions for success.

The myriad risks of turning an invention into an innovation contribute to business failures, but more importantly to underinvestment in commercial research and to opportunities foregone. Such lost opportunities are not restricted to would-be technical innovators—nor even to the trio of innovative actors made up of the inventor, the business executive, and the investor. Rather, the lost opportunities touch a large array of participants in the process of innovation: from customers to suppliers; from partners to competitors; from educators to state governments, federal research resources, and government regulators.

In this context, we cannot help but ask: How relevant to technological innovation at the start of the twenty-first century is the standard distinction between the market (guided by the principle of profit maximization) and the government (guided by concern for the well-being of the nation, the desire for institutional or political self-preservation, or some combination thereof)? In the global economy of today (and the increasingly global economy of tomorrow), how useful is it to think of government simply "stepping in" to address market failures?

An alternative is to begin one's analysis of the government's role in the innovation system with a recognition of the following fundamental premises:

• The "private" and "public" sectors are inextricably linked within the innovation system, and always have been.

• The boundaries between public and private are unclear, and getting more so.

• Regardless of the success of public policy in addressing appropriability problems, a network of well-functioning institutions (both private and public) is a prerequisite to the sort of ongoing, science-based innovation on which long-term economic growth is based.

• Increasingly, the success of the private, innovation-based economy depends on the complex network of relationships we called social capital. Public policy at the local, state, and federal levels is an important influence on the environment for innovation, but does not directly control it. Thus the role required of government, at all levels, is far more subtle and sophisticated than it was in an era when national security issues drove national policy.

Of course, fostering innovation and entrepreneurship is not a natural role for government. As Nathan Rosenberg and L. E. Birdzell, Jr., recognized in their classic book *How the West Grew Rich*, "In all well-ordered societies, political authority is dedicated to stability, security, and the status quo. It is thus singularly ill-qualified to direct or channel activity intended to produce instability, insecurity and change" (Rosenberg and Birdzell, 1985: 265).

Nevertheless, promoting innovation and entrepreneurship is increasingly seen as a pro-active responsibility of government. This is particularly so for the governments of the states. Government's most obvious and compelling role is the sponsorship or—when working with firms—co-sponsorship of advanced research with large potential for diffusion and further application. The federal government is relatively comfortable with the research supporting role. However, government tends to support only basic research except when it is the customer for the products that might result (notably, in military procurement) or when there is some other compelling government mission. There is a serious gap between the scientific support of federal agencies and the research needed to extend conceptual ideas for new products to the knowledge required for acceptable designs and processes, from which commercial products can be derived.

This gap is well illustrated by the two cases we analyzed earlier in this book. David Edwards, the inventor whose work led to the AIR company, spent four years after his commercial idea was in hand struggling for funding to prepare the technology to the point where investors would take it seriously. He used funding given him by Pennsylvania State University to set up his laboratory when he moved from MIT to accept a professorship there. Almost a decade elapsed before the inventions of Nam Suh resulted in the viable Trexel company. This research was financed in part by small grants from interested firms that thought they might become Trexel's customers in the future. These two cases suggest a role for government: the sponsorship of "downstream" research on the campus that would allow scientists and engineers with promising ideas to bring them closer to commercialization than is possible with most sources of academic research funding.

Beyond Schumpeter: Creative Destruction as a Public Imperative

In this volume we have repeatedly referred to the insights of economist Joseph Schumpeter, whose work on entrepreneurship and innovation (Schumpeter 1912, 1942), have provided the intellectual framework within which discourse on these topics continues to take place. He keenly perceived the role of the entrepreneur in forcing the "creative destruction" of existing modes of economic activity. At a relatively early stage he noted the gradual routinization of innovation that we emphasized at the beginning of this chapter, writing that "innovation itself is being reduced to routine. Technological progress in increasingly becoming the business of teams of trained specialists who turn out what is required and make it work in predictable ways" (Schumpeter 1942: 132). Yet one of the most striking, and least discussed, aspects of the Schumpeterian legacy is that the core thesis of Schumpeter's most celebrated work has now been shown to be absolutely and demonstrably wrong. Schumpeter (1942: 134) wrote:

Since capitalist enterprise, by its very achievements, tends to automatize progress, we conclude that it tends to make itself superfluous—to break to pieces under the pressure of its own success. The perfectly bureaucratized giant industrial unit not only ousts the small or medium-sized firm and "expropriates" its owners, but in the end it also ousts the entrepreneur and expropriates the bourgeoisie as a class which in the process stands to lose not only its income, but also what is infinitely more important, its function.

From the standpoint of the start of the twenty-first century—the age of Internet start-ups, 401K plans, incubators, and venture capitalists—this sweeping historical analysis is nothing more than a quaint reminder of the fixations of a century now passed. Yet we have as much to learn from the great theorist's misjudgments regarding the economic system as we do from his much better-publicized insights.

What has saved us from the calamity that Schumpeter foretold? Are large corporations not major players in the innovation process, at least in their core businesses? As we discussed at the start of Chapter III, the evidence is mixed. Large corporations and their affiliated research labs do, however, clearly play an important role in the innovation system. Is it not true that innovation has become more scientific, if not more manageable? We have already said that we see this to be the case. Then why has the entrepreneur not been displaced? Why do we observe technological "creative destruction" occurring at a rate far greater today then when Schumpeter wrote sixty years ago?

The answer is straightforward: Institutions and behavior have evolved and adapted to changing circumstances. As a result, individual inventors as well as corporations have as great an incentive today as ever to take the technical risks required to traverse the space between invention and innovation, and subsequently to endure the market risks required to bring a radical innovation to market.

The evolution of institutions has not been accidental. Leadership—that of corporations, financiers, and government officials—has been required at every stage. The postwar start-ups, such as Intel and Hewlett Packard, defied expectations to become giant companies while retaining their creative, entrepreneurial spirit, setting a pattern for others. The best of the venture firms were able, through their trusted networks, to identify innovators and nurture their ambitions. Government officials gave us the Bayh-Dole Act, which unleashed the entrepreneurial talents of the universities. The managers of DARPA showed how radical but high-risk technologies could be brought to fruition for government use. Visionaries like Mary Good sought to convince members of Congress of the legitimacy of a federal role in promoting commercial innovation, and governors like Richard Celeste of Ohio and Dick Thornburgh of Pennsylvania demonstrated the strong role state governments can play in promoting science-based innovation. Yet our exploration of the uncertainties associated with commercializing science-based ideas demonstrates that there are serious needs for additional institutional innovation—in the financial world, in the universities, in scientific research communities, and in the government agencies that support them.

In the coming century, creative destruction will continue to be a public as well as a private imperative. Yet we must recognize a serious political obstacle: the strong reluctance of some to having the federal government share private firms' costs for early-stage, research-based innovations. Schumpeter's phrase "creative destruction" carries with it the implication that whenever there are innovation winners, there are likely to be losers—losers who may complain to their political representatives if government agencies are seen as the instruments of their destruction, however creative it might be for the economy as a whole. But we believe that there is increasing recognition that government, when following an appropriately constrained role in the innovation process, is a legitimate, even necessary part of the national system of innovation. A dialogue between public and private leaders, experienced in the art of science-based innovation, is required to refine that role.

The innovation system in the United States today is, by any measure, a legitimate wonder of the world, despite the gaps and barriers discussed in this book. It could be even more successful if these institutional deficiencies were ameliorated. This is all the more reason for Americans to invest the energies and resources required today to ensure continued innovative productivity for at least a century to come.

Notes

1. For this reason the definition of invention as an idea protectable by a government patent has become less clearly distinguishable from other commercial ideas for which novel forms of intellectual property protection are increasingly sought.

2. "An *innovation* is the application of technical and/or marketing ingenuity to the creation of a new or improved product, process, or service that is successfully introduced into the market.... Relatively few *inventions* become *innovations.*" (Alic et al. 1992: 43). Richard R. Nelson (1993: 4) notes that an innovation does not have to be new to the world, only new to the firm.

3. Scientists over 70 years of age will well remember the situation in 1945. Only the simplest atom (hydrogen) could be quantitatively understood. Mathematical physics could deal only approximately with atoms with three or more particles. This meant that chemistry was largely confined to simple rules of valence taken from the recently filled-in periodic table of the elements, and simple symmetry rules for predicting chemical reactions. Biology was almost entirely descriptive. Engineers took pride in distinguishing their art from science, noting that they "learned by doing"; their empirical knowledge was based on experience and trial-and-error. The transition from that primitive time to our own, within the span of a single career, is nothing less than mind-boggling.

4. See also Branscomb, Kodama, and Florida (1999) and Thursby and Thursby (2000).

5. The concept of a national system of innovation (Nelson 1993) includes the "economic policies, institutional capacities, human resources, and their fruitful interactions" and is quite similar to the notion of social capital for innovation.

6. An example could be the competition between the Xerox Dynabook and the currently successful Palm Pilot.

7. Branstetter also presents comparable numbers for Stanford. The percentages are somewhat lower for research universities not associated with medical schools (most notably, MIT).

8. Of course, as Joy (2000) reminds us, we can fully expect innovation to continually create new threats just as it creates new opportunities. In this new century, managing the national security and public health risks of new technologies will be an increasingly important public policy challenge—but not one that should be confused with management of public support for the innovation system.

9. A detailed analysis of both input and output indicators of technology-based economic development, state by state, is given by the U. S. Department of Commerce's Office of Technology Policy (2000b).

10. ATP funding is intended to help firms extend the reach of their research back toward more speculative and basic research. While universities can participate as joint venture artners with commercial firms, ATP is not authorized to directly address the difficulty universities face in extending their basic research toward commercializable technology without the particiation of at least two commercial partners. This makes it more difficult for ATP to assist university researchers trying to bridge the R&D gap in order to start up a new firm not yet in existence.

11. We might characterize the failure of supply-and-demand-side policies to be balanced and harmonized as another gap—the innovation policy gap.

12. Rick Burnes of Charles River Ventures notes that opportunities for radical, science-based innovations are still rare, compared to the new possibilities from steadily evolving advanced technologies. "The problem is today that a lot of the projects that come in don't have any real differentiation. That is a shift from the environment that we were in, in the 1970s and 1980s, where we did see a lot of technically sophisticated projects, where there was technical risk and we took that risk. In fact, I would say that we may very well be going through a phase in the evolution of venture capital where there are many, many opportunities that the existing technologies can address and create major companies."

References

Acs, Z. J. and D. B. Audretsch. 1988. "Innovation in Large and Small Firms: An Empirical Analysis," *American Economic Review* 78: 678–690.

Alic, John A., Lewis M. Branscomb, Harvey Brooks, Ashton B. Carter, and Gerald L. Epstein. 1992. *Beyond Spinoff: Military and Commercial Technologies in a Changing World.* Boston: Harvard Business School Press.

Aghion, Philippe and Jean Tirole. 1994. "The Management of Innovation," *Quarterly Journal of Economics* 109(4): 1185–1209.

Amram, Martha and Nalin Kulatilaka. 1999. *Real Options: Managing Strategic Investment in an Uncertain World.* Boston: Harvard University Press.

Arrow, Kenneth J. 1962. "Economic welfare and the allocation of resources from invention," in *The Rate and Direction of Inventive Activity: Economic and Social Factors.* Princeton, NJ: Princeton University Press.

Arthur, W. B. 1989. "Competing technologies, increasing returns and lock-in by historical events," *Economic Journal* 99: 116–131.

Arthur D. Little, Inc. 1958. "Report to International Business Machines Corporation: Investigation of Two Haloid-Xerox Machines as New Product Opportunities in the Office Reproducing Equipment Field," 1 December [C-61613]. Cambridge, MA: A. D. Little.

Auerswald, Philip, Stuart Kauffman, José Lobo, and Karl Shell. 2000. "The Production Recipes Approach to Modeling Technological Innovation: An Application to Learning by Doing," *Journal of Economic Dynamics and Control* 24: 389–450.

Bain, Joe S. 1956. *Barriers to New Competition.* Cambridge, MA: Harvard University Press.

Baumol, William J. 1993. *Entrepreneurship, Management, and the Structure of Payoff.* Cambridge, MA: MIT Press.

Brandenburger, Adam M. and Barry J. Nalebuff. 1997. *Co-opetition.* New York: Doubleday.

Branscomb, Lewis M. 1986. "IBM and U.S. Universities—An Evolving Partnership," *IEEE Transactions on Education* E-29 (2): 69–77.

Branscomb, Lewis M. 1989. "From Science Policy to Research Policy," in Lewis M. Branscomb and James Keller, eds. *Investing in Innovation: Creating a Research and Innovation Policy that Works.* Cambridge, MA: MIT Press.

Branscomb, Lewis M. 1996. "Social Capital: the Key Element in Science-Based Development," *Annals of the N.Y. Academy of Science* 798 (18 December): 1–8.

Branscomb, Lewis M. and Young Hwan Choi. 1996. *Korea at the Turning Point.* Greenwich, CT: Praeger Press.

Branscomb, Lewis M. and James Keller, eds. 1998. *Investing in Innovation: Creating a Research and Innovation Policy that Works.* Cambridge, MA: MIT Press.

Branscomb, Lewis M., and Fumio Kodama, 1993. *Japanese Innovation Strategy: Technical Support for Business Visions.* CSIA Occasional Paper Series. Lanham, MD: University Press of America.

Branscomb, Lewis M., Fumio Kodama, and Richard Florida, eds. 1999. *Industrializing Knowledge: University-Industry Linkages in Japan and the United States.* Cambridge, MA: MIT Press.

Branscomb, Lewis M., Kenneth Morse, and Michael Roberts. 2000. *Managing Technical Risk: Understanding Private Sector Decision Making on Early Stage, Technology-Based Projects.* Advanced Technology Program, National Institute for Standards and Technology, US Department of Commerce, NIST GCR 00-787, April 2000. <http://www.atp.nist.gov/eao/gcr_787.pdf>

Branstetter, Lee. 2000. "Measuring the Link Between Academic Science and Industrial Innovation: The Case of California's Research Universities," unpublished mimeograph.

Burback, Ron. 1998. Home page: <www-db.stanford.edu/%7Eburback>

Candell, Amy B. and Adam Jaffe. 1999. "The Regional Economic Impact of Public Research Funding: A Case Study in Massachusetts," in Lewis Branscomb, Fumio Kodama, and Richard Florida, eds., *Industrializing Knowledge: University-Industry Linkages in Japan and the United States.* Cambridge, MA: MIT Press.

Christensen, Clayton M. 1997. *The Innovator's Dilemma: When New Technologies Cause Great Firms to Fail.* Boston: Harvard Business School Press.

Christensen, Clayton M., and Richard S. Rosenbloom. 1995. "Explaining the Attacker's Advantage," *Research Policy* 24: 233–257.

Cockburn, Ian M., Rebecca Henderson, and Scott Stern. 1999. "The Diffusion of Science Driven Drug Discovery: Organizational Change in the Pharmaceutical Industry," NBER Working Paper 7359.

Cohan, Peter. 1999. *Net Profit: How to Invest and Compete in the Real World of Internet Business.* San Francisco: Jossey-Bass.

Council on Competitiveness. 1998. *Going Global: The New Shape of American Innovation.* Washington, DC: Council on Competitiveness.

Dasgupta, Partha and Eric Maskin. 1987. "The Simple Economics of Research Portfolios," *The Economic Journal* 97(387): 581–595.

Dernburg, T. and N. Gharrity. 1961–1962. "A statistical analysis of patent renewal data for three countries," *Patent, Trademark, and Copyright Journal* 5: 340–361.

Dertouzos, Michael L., Robert M. Solow, and Robert Lester. 1989. *Made in America: Regaining the Productive Edge*. Cambridge, MA: MIT Press.

Dixit, Avinash K. 1981. "The role of investment in entry deterrence," *Economic Journal* 90(357): 95–106 (March).

Dixit, A and R. Pindyck. 1994. *Investment under Uncertainty*. Princeton: Princeton University Press.

Ehlers, Vernon J. 1998. *Unlocking our Future: Toward a New National Science Policy. A Report to Congress by the House Committee on Science*. Washington, DC: Government Printing Office.

Ergas, Henry. 1989. "Global Technology and National Politics," Unpublished paper for the Council on Foreign Relations, New York, 26 June 1989.

Etzkowitz, Henry. 1989. "The Second Academic Revolution: The Role of the Research University in Economic Development," in Susan E. Cozzens, Peter Healey, Arie Rip, and John Ziman, eds. *The Research System in Transition*, NATO ASI Series. Dordrecht: Kluwer Academic Publishers.

Etzkowitz, Henry. 1999. "Bridging the Gap: The Evolution of Industry-University Links in the United States," in Lewis M. Branscomb, Fumio Kodama, and Richard Florida, eds. *Industrializing Knowledge: University-Industry Linkages in Japan and the United States*. Cambridge, MA: MIT Press.

Evenson, Robert E. and Yoav Kislev. 1976. "A stochastic model of applied research," *Journal of Political Economy* 84(2): 265–82.

Feynman, Richard P. 1989. *What Do You Care What Other People Think? Further Adventures of a Curious Character*. New York: W.W. Norton Company.

Fogarty, Michael S., and Amit K. Sinha. 1999. "Why Older Regions Can't Generalize from Route 128 and Silicon Valley," in Lewis M. Branscomb, Fumio Kodama, and Richard Florida, eds. *Industrializing Knowledge: University-Industry Linkages in Japan and the United States*. Cambridge, MA: MIT Press.

Foster, Richard N. 1986. *Innovation: The Attacker's Advantage*. New York: Summit Books.

Fountain, Jane. 1998. "Social Capital: A Key Enabler of Innovation," in Lewis M. Branscomb and James Keller, eds. *Investing in Innovation: Creating a Research and Innovation Policy that Works*. Cambridge, MA: MIT Press.

Gans, Joshua S., David H. Hsu, and Scott Stern. 2000. "When Does Start-up Innovation Spur the Gale of Creative Destruction?" Washington, D.C.: NBER Working Paper 7851.

Gardiner, G. E. 1997. "Strategies for Technology Development: A Presentation to the Board of the Yale Corporation." <http://www.yale.edu/ocr/yalecorp.html>

Gompers, P. A. 1995. "Optimal Investment, monitoring and the staging of venture capital," *Journal of Finance* 50: 1461–1489.

Gompers, P.A. and J. Lerner. 1999. *The Venture Capital Cycle.* Cambridge: MIT Press.

Grabowski, H. and J. Vernon. 1990. "A new look at the returns and risks to pharmaceutical R&D," *Management Science* 36: 804–821.

Grabowski, H. and J. Vernon. 1994. "Returns on new drug introductions in the 1980s," *Journal of Health Economics* 13: 383–406.

Grabowski, H. and J. Vernon. 1996. "Prospects for returns to pharmaceutical R&D under health care reform," in R. Helms, ed., *Competitive Strategies in the Pharmaceutical Industry.* Washington, DC: American Enterprise Institute.

Griliches, Zvi. 1992. "The Search for R&D Spillovers," *Scandinavian Journal of Economics* 94: S29–S47.

Gundlach, Robert W. 1988. "Xerography from the Beginning," *Xerox World* 7(3) (Fall/Winter): 6–9.

Harhoff, D., F. Narin, F. M. Scherer, and K. Vopel. 1999. "Citation frequency and value of patented inventions," *Review of Economics and Statistics* 81: 511–515.

Harhoff, D., F.M. Scherer, and K. Vopel. 1997. "Exploring the tail of patent value distributions." Mannheim: Center for European Economic Research Discussion Paper No. 97-30.

Hart, David M. 1998. "Managing Technology Policy in the White House," in Lewis M. Branscomb and James Keller, eds. *Investing in Innovation: Creating a Research and Innovation Policy that Works.* Cambridge, MA: MIT Press.

Hartmann, George C. and Andras I. Lakatos. 1998. "Assessing Technology Risk: A Case Study," *Journal of Research Technology Management* 32 (April–May).

Henderson, Rebecca and Iain Cockburn. 1996. "Scale, Scope, and Spillovers: The Determinants of Research Productivity in Drug Discovery," *Rand Journal of Economics* 27(1): 32–59.

Hill, Christopher. 1998. "The Advanced Technology Program: Opportunities for Enhancement," in Lewis M. Branscomb and James Keller, eds. *Investing in Innovation: Creating a Research and Innovation Policy that Works.* Cambridge, MA: MIT Press.

Hounshell, David A. and John Kenly Smith, Jr. 1988. *Science and Corporate Strategy: DuPont R&D, 1902–1980.* Cambridge: Cambridge University Press.

Huchzermeier, A. and C. H. Loch. 1999. "Project Management Under Risk: Using the Real Options Approach to Evaluate Flexibility in R&D," INSEAD Working Paper 99/15/TM.

Jaffe, Adam. 2000. "The U.S. patent system in transition: policy innovation and the innovation process," *Research Policy* 29: 531–557.

Jones, Charles I. and John C. Williams. 1998. "Measuring the Social Returns to R&D," *Quarterly Journal of Economics* 113(4): 1119–1135 (November).

Joy, Bill. 2000. "Why the future doesn't need us." *Wired* 8(4), April.

Judd, Kenneth L. 1998. *Numerical Methods in Economics.* Cambridge, MA: MIT Press.

Kennedy, Carol. 1989. "Xerox Charts a New Direction," *Long Range Planning* 22 (1): 10–17.

Kirzner, Israel M. 1973. *Competition and Entrepreneurship.* Chicago: University of Chicago Press.

Knight, Frank. 1921. *Risk and Uncertainty.* New York: Houghton Mifflin Company.

Kortum, Samuel and Josh Lerner. 1999. "What is behind the recent surge in patenting?" *Research Policy* 28(1): 1–22.

Krueger, Alan B. and Timothy Taylor. 2000. "An Interview of Zvi Griliches," *Journal of Economic Perspectives* 14 (2).

Kukies, J., Scherer, F.M., 1998. "Zeit fur wirtschafts und finanzpragmatischen transfer: Das innovationsverhalten deutscher und amerikanischer unternehmen," in S. Lorenz and M. Machill, eds., *Transatlantischer Transfer von Politik, Wirtschaft und Kultur.* Opladen: Westdeutscher Verlag.

Kuznets, Simon S. 1930. *Secular Movements in Production and Prices: Their Nature and their Bearing Upon Cyclical Fluctuations.* Boston: Houghton Mifflin Company.

Laffont, Jean-Jacques. 1990. *The Economics of Uncertainty and Information.* Cambridge MA: MIT Press.

Lanjouw, J. O. and M. Shankerman. 1997. "Stylized Facts of Patent Litigation: Value, Scope and Ownership," NBER Working Paper 6287. Washington, D. C. National Bureau of Economic Research.

Lerner, Josh. 1999. "Venture Capital and the Commercialization of Academic Technology: Symbiosis and Paradox," in Lewis M. Branscomb, Fumio Kodama, and Richard Florida, eds. *Industrializing Knowledge: University-Industry Linkages in Japan and the United States.* Cambridge, MA: MIT Press.

Lerner, Josh. 2000. "When Bureaucrats Meet Entrepreneurs: The Design of Effective 'Public Venture Capital'," In Lewis M. Branscomb, Kenneth Morse, and Michael Roberts, *Managing Technical Risk: Understanding Private Sector Decision Making on Early Stage, Technology-Based Projects.* Advanced Technology Program, National Institute for Standards and Technology, US Department of Commerce, NIST GCR 00-787, April 2000. <http://www.atp.nist.gov/eao/gcr_787.pdf>

Lewis, David. 2000. "Technical Risk and the Mid-Sized Company," in Lewis M. Branscomb, Kenneth Morse, and Michael Roberts, *Managing Technical Risk: Understanding Private Sector Decision Making on Early Stage, Technology-Based Projects.* Advanced Technology Program, National Institute for Standards and Technology, US Department of Commerce, NIST GCR 00-787, April 2000. <http://www.atp.nist.gov/eao/gcr_787.pdf>

Lippman, S. and R. Rumelt. 1982. "Uncertain imitability: An analysis of interfirm differences in efficiency under competition," *The Bell Journal of Economics* 13: 418–438.

Loch, C. and K. Bode-Greuel. 2000. "Expansion Options: Evaluating Strategic Opportunities from Research Projects." Fontainebleau: INSEAD Working Paper 2000/13/TM.

Mansfield, Edwin. 1985. "How rapidly does new industrial technology leak out?" *Journal of Industrial Economics* 34(2): 217–223 (December).

Mansfield, Edwin, John Rapoport, Anthony Remeo, Samuel Wagner and George Beardsley. 1977. "Social and Private Returns from Industrial Innovations," *Quarterly Journal of Economics*, 91(2): 221–240 (May).

McColough, Peter C. 1984. "The Birth of Xerox," *Agenda* 20 (May). Rochester, N.Y.: Xerox Corporation.

McGrath, Michael E., Michael T. Anthony, and Amram R. Shapiro. 1992. *Product Development, Success Through Product and Cycle-time Excellence.* Newton, MA: Butterworth-Heinemann Press.

Morgenthaler, David. 2000. "Assessing Technical Risk," in Lewis M. Branscomb, Kenneth Morse, and Michael Roberts. *Managing Technical Risk: Understanding Private Sector Decision Making on Early Stage, Technology-Based Projects.* Advanced Technology Program, National Institute for Standards and Technology, US Department of Commerce, NIST GCR 00-787, April 2000. <http://www.atp.nist.gov/eao/gcr_787.pdf>

Mowery, David C., Richard Nelson, Bhaven N. Sampat, and Arvids A. Ziedonis. 1999. "The Effects of the Bayh Dole Act on U.S. University Research and Technology Transfer," in Lewis M. Branscomb, Fumio Kodama, and Richard Florida, eds. *Industrializing Knowledge: University-Industry Linkages in Japan and the United States.* Cambridge, MA: MIT Press.

Myers, Mark B. 1996. "Research and Change Management in Xerox," in Richard S. Rosenbloom and William J. Spencer, eds., *Engines of Innovation: U.S. Industrial Research at the End of an Era.* Boston: Harvard Business School Press.

National Research Council, Board on Science, Technology, and Economic Policy. 1999. *The Small Business Innovation Research Program SBIR: Challenges and Opportunities.* Washington DC: National Academy Press.

Nelson, Richard R. 1959. "The Simple Economics of Scientific Research," *Journal of Political Economy* 68 (3): 297–306.

Nelson, Richard R., ed. 1993. *National Innovation Systems: A Comparative Analysis.* New York: Oxford University Press.

Nordhaus, W. D. 1989. Comment. *Brookings Papers on Economic Activity. Microeconomics:* 320–325.

Nordhaus, W.D. 1997. "Do real output and real wage measures capture reality?" in T. Bresnahan and R. J. Gordon, eds. *The Economics of New Goods.* Chicago: University of Chicago Press.

Office of Technology Policy. 2000a. U.S. Department of Commerce. *Tech Transfer 2000: Making Parnerships Work.* (May).

Office of Technology Policy. 2000b. U.S. Department of Commerce. *The Dynamics of Technology-based Economic Development: State Science and Technology Indicators.* (June).

Pakes, A. 1986. "Patents as options: Some estimates of the value of holding European patent stocks," *Econometrica* 54: 755–784.

Pakes, A. and M. Schankerman. 1984. "The rate of obsolescence of patents, research gestation lags, and the private rate of return to research resources," in Z. Griliches, ed., *R&D, Patents, and Productivity.* Chicago: University of Chicago Press.

Peck, M. J., and F. M. Scherer. 1962. *The Weapons Acquisition Process: An Economic Analysis.* Boston: Harvard Business School Division of Research.

Pell, Eric. 1998. *From Dream to Riches—The Story of Xerography* (privately printed).

Price Waterhouse Coopers. 2000. <www.pricewaterhouse.com>.

Ravenscraft, D. and F. M. Scherer. 1982. "The lag structure of returns to R&D," *Applied Economics* 25: 603–620.

Rhodes, Richard. 1999. *Visions of Technology: A Century of Vital Debate about Machines, Systems, and the Human World.* New York: Simon & Schuster.

Roberts, Michael J. and Diana Gardner. 1999. *Advanced Inhalation Research, Inc.* Harvard Business School Case No. 9-899-292.

Roberts, Michael J. and Matthew C. Lieb. 1999. *Trexel.* Harvard Business School Case No. 9-899-101.

Rosenberg, Nathan and L.E. Birdzell, Jr. 1985. *How the West Grew Rich: The Economic Transformation of the Industrial World.* New York: Basic Books.

Roussel, Phillip A., Kamal N. Saad, and Tamara J. Erickson. 1991. *Third Generation R&D: Managing the Link to Corporate Strategy.* Boston: Harvard Business School Press.

Schankerman, M. and A. Pakes. 1986. "Estimates of the value of patent rights in European Countries during the post-1950 period," *Economic Journal* 97: 1–25.

Scherer, F.M. 1965. "Firm size, market structure, opportunity, and the output of patented inventions," *American Economic Review* 55: 1097–1123.

Scherer, F. M. 1984. *Innovation and growth: Schumpeterian perspectives.* Cambridge, MA: MIT Press.

Scherer, F.M. 1992. "Schumpeter and plausible capitalism," *Journal of Economic Literature* 30: 1416–1433.

Scherer, F.M. 1996. Commentary, in R. Helms, ed. , *Competitive Strategies in the Pharmaceutical Industry.* Washington DC: American Enterprise Institute.

Scherer, F.M. 1998. "The size distribution of profits from innovation," *Annales d'Economie et de Statistique* 49/50: 495–516.

Scherer, F. M. 1999. *New Perspectives on Economic Growth and Technological Innovation.* Washington, DC: The Brookings Institution.

Scherer, F.M., D. Harhoff, and J. Kukies. 2000. "Uncertainty and the size distribution of rewards from technological innovation," *Journal of Evolutionary Economics* 10(1/2): 175–200.

Schmalensee. Richard. 1981. "Economies of scale and barriers to entry," *Journal of Political Economy* 89(6): 1228–1238 (December).

Schmalensee, Richard. 1982. "Product differentiation advantages of pioneering brands," *American Economic Review* 72(3): 349–365.

Schmookler, J. 1966. *Invention and Economic Growth.* Cambridge, MA: Harvard University Press.

Schumpeter, Joseph A. 1912. *Theorie der witschaftlichen Entwicklung.* Leipzig: Duncker & Humblot. Revised English translation (1934) by Redvers Opie, *The Theory of Economic Development.* Oxford: Oxford University Press.

Schumpeter, Joseph A. 1942. *Capitalism, Socialism and Democracy.* New York: Harper & Brothers.

Shane, Scott. 2000. "Technology Regime and New Firm Formation," in Lewis M. Branscomb, Kenneth Morse, and Michael Roberts. *Managing Technical Risk: Understanding Private Sector Decision Making on Early Stage, Technology-Based Projects.* Advanced Technology Program, National Institute for Standards and Technology, US Department of Commerce, NIST GCR 00-787, April 2000. <http://www.atp.nist.gov/eao/gcr_787.pdf>

Shell, Karl. 1966. "Toward a theory of inventive activity and capital accumulation," *American Economic Review* 56(2): 62–68.

Shell. Karl. 1973. "Inventive activity, industrial organisation and economic growth." In J. A. Mirrlees and N. H. Stern, eds., *Models of Economic Growth.* John Wiley and Sons.

Smiley, R. H. and S. A. Ravid. 1983. "The importance of being first: Learning price and strategy," *Quarterly Journal of Economics* May: 353–362.

Smith, Preston G. and Donald G. Reinertsen. 1998. *Developing Products in Half the Time,* 2d ed. New York: John Wiley & Sons.

Smith, Lee. 1980. "A Miracle in Search of a Market," *Fortune,* 1 December, pp. 92–95.

Spence, Michael. 1984. "Cost Reduction, Competition, and Industry Performance," *Econometrica* 52(1): 101–121.

State Science and Technology Institute. 1996. *State Funding for Cooperative Technology Programs.* Columbus, OH: SSTI (June).

State Science and Technology Institute. 1999. *State and Federal Perspectives on the SBIR Program,* prepared for the U.S. Innovation Partnership SBIR Task Force, 614/901-1690. Westerville, OH: SSTI.

Sutton, John. 1991. *Sunk Costs and Market Structure: Price Competition, Advertising and the Evolution of Concentration.* Cambridge MA: MIT Press.

Tassey, Greg. 1999. *R&D Trends in the U.S. Economy: Strategies and Policy Implications.* Washington, D.C.: U.S. Department of Commerce, Technology Administration, National Institute of Standards and Technology.

Teece, David. 1987. "Capturing Value for Technology Innovation: Innovation, Integration, Strategic Partnering and Licensing Decisions," In B. R. Guile and H. Brooks, eds. *Technology and Global Industry: Companies and Nations in the World Economy.* Washington, DC: National Academy Press.

Thursby, J. G. and M. C. Thursby, 2000. "Who is Selling the Ivory Tower? Sources of Growth in University Licensing," NBER Working Paper 7718. Washington, DC: National Bureau of Economic Research.

U.S. National Science Board. 1998. *Science and Engineering Indicators 1998.* Arlington, VA: NSB 98-1.

U.S. National Science Board. 2000. *Science and Engineering Indicators 2000.* Washington, DC: National Science Foundation.

Utterback, James. 1994. *Mastering the Dynamics of Innovation: How Companies Can Seize Opportunities in the Face of Technological Change.* Boston: Harvard Business School Press.

Vest, Charles M. 2000. "Science, Technology, and Innovation: Reflections on Change," in Albert H. Teich, Stephen D. Nelson, Ceilia McEnaney and Stephen J. Lita, eds., *AAAS Science and Technology Policy Yearbook 2000.* Washington DC: American Association for the Advancement of Science, pp. 317–327.

Watson, Thomas J. 2000. *Father, Son and Co: My Life at IBM And Beyond,* New York: Random House.

About the Contributors

Philip E. Auerswald is a postdoctoral fellow in the Belfer Center for Science and International Affairs at Harvard University's Kennedy School of Government. His research focuses on the economics of technological change, industrial organization, and international political economy. Since 1995 he has been the editor of the *Foreign Policy Bulletin* (published by Kluwer Law International).

Lewis M. Branscomb is Aetna Professor of Public Policy and Corporate Management, emeritus, and Emeritus Director of the Science, Technology and Public Policy Program in the Belfer Center for Science and International Affairs at Harvard University's Kennedy School of Government. He is Principal Investigator of the Harvard Information Infrastructure Project and other projects in Technology Policy in the Center. A research physicist at the U.S. National Bureau of Standards (now the National Institute of Standards and Technology) from 1951 to 1969, he was Director of NBS from 1969 to 1972. In 1972 Dr. Branscomb was named Vice President and Chief Scientist of IBM Corporation and appointed to its Management Committee, serving until his retirement from IBM in 1986. While at IBM, he was appointed by President Carter to the National Science Board and in 1980 was elected chairman, serving until May 1984. He is co-editor of *Investing in Innovation*, published in 1998, and *Industrializing Knowledge*, in 1999.

Henry Chesbrough is an assistant professor of business administration, and the Class of 1961 Fellow, at Harvard Business School. His research focuses on institutions and innovation, and on technology venturing. Prior to embarking on an academic career, he spent ten years in various product planning and strategic marketing positions in Silicon Valley companies. He worked for seven of those years at Quantum Corporation, a leading hard disk drive manufacturer and a Fortune 500 company. He was Vice President of Marketing and Business Development for Plus Development Corporation, an entrepreneurial subsidiary of Quantum.

Mary L. Good is the Donaghey University Professor at the University of Arkansas, Little Rock, and serves as Interim Dean for the College of Information Science and Systems Engineering. She is also president-elect of the American Association for the Advancement of Science. Previously, she was the Under Secretary for Technology for the Technology Administration in the Department of Commerce. Dr. Good also chaired the National Science and Technology Council's Committee on Technological Innovation and coordinated the Clinton Administration's Partnership for a New Generation of Vehicles effort.

Dietmar Harhoff is director of the Institute of Innovation Research and Technology Management, University of Munich, and is a professor in the Faculty of Business Administration. His research interests are in the area of industrial economics, and in particular in technological innovation, productivity, and human capital formation.

George C. Hartmann is a former principal in the Strategy and Innovation Group, concerned with technology strategies for Xerox Corporate Research and Technology. During thirty-one years with Xerox, he contributed to research on novel marking systems, managed advanced technology groups dealing with development of xerographic subsystems for new products, and contributed to technical planning.

James C. McGroddy retired from IBM as a Senior Vice President at the end of 1996, after leading its research laboratories from 1989 to 1995. He currently serves as Chairman of the Board of Integrated Surgical Systems, a public company bringing robotic technology to the operating room, and is involved in the restructuring of the local health care system in Westchester County. During his career at IBM, he drove significant change in the structure of relations between IBM's research efforts and commercialization. In at least a few cases he was instrumental in his drive to create new commercial entities, the largest being DTI, a joint venture between Toshiba and IBM which is one of the world's leading suppliers of flat-panel displays.

Mark B. Myers retired in August 2000 from the position of senior vice president of research and technology at the Xerox Corporation, where he directed the company's worldwide research, advanced development, technical architecture, and corporate engineering. His technical and management interests included digital imaging systems and the creation of new technical and business enterprises involving emerging areas of technology. He has developed new models for innovation systems in industry and their relationships to universities and government. He currently co-chairs with Richard Levin, the president of Yale University, the NRC Science, Technology and Economic Policy (STEP) Board's study of the U.S. Intellectual Property System.

Richard S. Rosenbloom is the David Sarnoff Professor of Business Administration, emeritus, at Harvard Business School, where he taught courses on Manufacturing Management, Innovation, and Technology and Competitive Strategy from 1958 to 1997. Professor Rosenbloom was co-editor of and contributor to *Engines of Innovation: U.S. Industrial Research at the End of an Era* (HBS Press 1996). Other recent writings include "Rethinking the Role of Industrial Research" (*Research Technology Management*), "The Transformation of Industrial Research" (*Issues in Science and Technology*), "Explaining the Attacker's Advantage" (*Research Policy*) and "Technological Discontinuities, Organizational Capabilities, and Strategic Commitments" (*Industrial and Corporate Change*).

Frederic M. Scherer is Aetna Professor of Public Policy and Corporate Management, emeritus, Kennedy School of Government, Harvard University. He has focused his research on two main themes: industrial organization economics and the economics of technological change. His publications include several books: *International High-Technology Competition; New Perspectives on Eco-*

nomic Growth and Technological Innovation; *The Weapons Acquisition Process*; *Mergers, Sell-Offs and Economic Efficiency*; *Innovation and Growth*; *The Economics of Multi-Plant Operation*; and *Competition Policies for an Integrated World Economy*, as well as two textbooks: *Industrial Market Structure and Economic Performance*; and a newer (1996) textbook, *Industry, Structure, Strategy, and Public Policy*. During the mid-1970s he was director of the Federal Trade Commission's Bureau of Economics. His current research is on the economics of the music composition "business" in the eighteenth century.

Index